On the Nature of Entrenched Prejudice

liverite Tony, I...find it dangerous that you say we can "choose" how we interpret the Scriptures. And sir, quite frankly, that's where you are just plain dangerous to the lives of others of what you're putting out there.

The points of views I'm expressing are not simply my own but the conclusions of numerous Biblical scholars...

pistol pete ...your main purpose...is a lingering battle over the homosexual marriage amendment to the constitution that you seek to have overturned.

And the arguments for that amendment were bigoted and fear based, and one day *will be* overturned...

koop Tony, your statements to defend your position are circular. When equality is agreed on to be a desirable state for everyone, but insisting on a label such as marriage for same sex unions, reveals your true motives...

So where is the equality when marriage is limited to heterosexual couples and gays get something else?...Would you be content if gays got to call it marriage and straights were granted civil unions under the conditions you would apply to gays?

pp Here's the only issue: You are trying to cause others to throw out two thousand years of scholarship and basic common sense because you say so.

Your argument...makes about as much sense as that of slave owners who made the same type of claims to justify their position. They used the Bible, too.

©2018
Upon My Word
Delaware, Ohio

On the Nature of Entrenched Prejudice

In 2002, an editorial I wrote was printed in the local newspaper. The premise of that article was that the Bible does not condemn homosexuality, and that the "clobber" verses used by many persons calling themselves Christians were lines taken out of their historical, cultural, and linguistic contexts. My conclusions were summarized this way:

Genesis 19:4-5 ([4]But before they lay down, the men of the city, even the men of Sodom, compassed the house round, both old and young, all the people from every quarter: [5]And they called unto Lot, and said unto him, Where are the men which came in to thee this night? bring them out unto us, that we may know them) **The story of Sodom is about attempted rape, not sexual orientation.**

Leviticus 18:22 and 20:13 ([22]Thou shalt not lie with mankind, as with womankind: it is abomination... [13]If a man also lie with mankind, as he lieth with a woman, both of them have committed an abomination: they shall surely be put to death; their blood shall be upon them.) **These verses are concerned with two Jewish men not procreating. Disobedience of this law was not a breach of morality but rather a violation of ritual. This law did not apply to Jewish women or to gentiles of either sex.**

Romans 1:22-27 ([22]Professing themselves to be wise, they became fools, [23]And changed the glory of the uncorruptible God into an image made like to corruptible man, and to birds, and four-footed beasts, and creeping things. [24]Wherefore God also gave them up to uncleanness through the lusts of their own hearts, to dishonor their own bodies between themselves... for even their women did change the natural use into that which is against nature: ^{27}And likewise also the men, leaving the natural use of the woman, burned in their lust one toward another; men with men working that which is unseemly, and receiving in themselves that recompense of their error which was meet.) **Paul decries idolatry, which he says has caused heterosexual women to act in sexually inappropriate ways and heterosexual men to indulge their lust. He says they act dishonorably but does not condemn them.**

I Corinthians 6:9-10 and I Timothy 1:9-10 (^{9}Know ye not that the unrighteous shall not inherit the kingdom of God? Be not deceived: neither fornicators, nor idolaters, nor adulterers, nor effeminate, nor abusers of themselves with mankind, ^{10}Nor thieves, nor covetous, nor drunkards, nor revilers, nor extortioners, shall inherit the kingdom of God...^{10}For whoremongers, for them that defile themselves with mankind, for men stealers, for liars, for perjured persons, and if there be any other thing that is contrary to sound doctrine...) **This is most likely a reference to male prostitution. Paul only refers to men and says nothing about lesbians, making it an improbable reference to orientation.**

Over the next six years, scores of criticisms and vehement rejections of my conclusions were published, and I continued to respond to these mostly extremist views, challenging their often homophobic and always heterosexist viewpoints. When attempts were made by certain state officials that would deny LGBT people their civil right to marry, I open criticized their efforts. When the Boy Scouts of America took discriminatory actions against gay Scouts and gay Scoutmasters, I worked to get the BSA dropped by United Way in my community. I responded to practically every printed argument and screed in several newspapers, and most of the time, my counterstatements were printed. I went so far as to make myself available for a debate, in a public forum that would be sponsored by the local town paper. After two weeks, there were no takers, and the only response the editor received was an anonymous e-mail that said, "He's a queer."

That was pretty much in keeping with the level of discourse I had come to expect from my critics. To illustrate this point, I offer the following letters as examples reflecting the mindsets and quality of the arguments anti-LGBT writers produced. Although the content of these missives is given verbatim, I've omitted the names of their authors in an effort to avoid opening old wounds for them now that same-sex marriage has been is legalized and the prejudices they openly displayed have come to be regarded by a majority of Americans as bigoted.

> Dear Editor:
> God's sexual preference is one man and one woman in a loving relationship. His orientation is that they are to be fruitful and multiply and replenish the earth.
> Eternity is coming for all of us. Don't you think it would be better for Mr. Marconi's neighbors to judge him and show him the error of his ways than for him to meet the judge at the great white throne of judgment with the books open?
> The 20th Century B.C. Sodomites did not seem to have any civil rights problems. They got together, both old and young, all the people from every quarter. They were having a great time until God put a stop to it.

> Dear Editor:
> Based on statements in Tony Marconi's [letter], he is a very liberal-minded Democrat. Only a true liberal would try to stand up for trying to teach the gay lifestyle to a classroom full of preschoolers. It is liberals like him who hand out condoms in schools. It is liberals like him who have *Janie has Two Mommies*

on shelves in our elementary schools. It is liberals like him who have dumbed-downed in school, and society in general, into thinking we should accept the gay lifestyle as perfectly normal. I, for one, am going to make a stand here and now for common decency. I do not and will never accept the gay lifestyle. Gays go against God, and nature, and everything taught to me from my youth.

If you are gay, keep it to yourself. Don't expect special privileges on the job because you sleep with someone of the same sex. Talk to a minister or priest and try to find God. Try to change your errant ways and align your will with God's will.

Mr. Marconi should write his vote-getting letters to the editor to back up concerned parents for their children. There are a lot more voters with concerned parents than there are with the gay community. He should have learned that from another liberal Democrat, Bill Clinton. Everything he does or says is for the children. Ha!

Dear Editor:
Hooray for any state representative who would introduce legislation to ban same-sex marriages. Along with civil rights we *all* have in this democracy, we should abide by majority rules.

It seems to me the homosexuals want me to condone their lifestyle by voting for someone who would pass legislation to let them marry each other. No way.

In the 1950s, heterosexuals I knew looked upon homosexual acts as being unnatural. That's how I feel about pedophiles today. It's unnatural. Pedophiles have a sexual orientation, too; does this give them full civil rights?

According to Tony Marconi's logic, it does. All we have to do is change the dictionary definition of "abnormal" to "sexual desire."

Just where are we headed 40 years from now. Will the speaker of the house be proud of his or her pedophile sibling

for coming out of the closet?
Think about it. It is up to the majority. Right?

By 2008, I had developed a talk entitled "God vs. Gays: The War That Never Was." I had already delivered this presentation at a couple of dozen colleges, universities, and churches, and I felt it was time to do so in my own town. I penned another letter to the editor inviting the public to the talk, and in the fall of that year, I sent yet another invitation via the editorial page asking the public to stop by either a festival booth in town a fair booth in another close-by community where I was active in the work of a gay-straight alliance. These three pieces sparked over 1,500 posts on two separate online chat threads.

I began engaging on the first of these threads in what I mistakenly assumed was a rational dialogue with a group of posting regulars who, with a few notable exceptions, turned out to have much to say but no willingness to listen to anything other than their own preconceptions. This book contains actual exchanges over an approximate eighteen-month period circa 2008-2010.

I have decided to compile and publish a portion of those postings because I think it important that a record be kept as to the type of arguments being made against the LGBT community at that time and of the mindsets of those making them. At that moment in history, the Q and I were not part of the shorthand employed in the struggle for human rights, but I suspect that the conversation would not have been much different if they had been.

To make the dialogue more distinguishable, I have kept my responses in bold font. I also changed the other posters' IDs (though none of the other contributors used their real names). I would be more than happy to give full credit to any of them if they ever choose to come forward. I have met a few of those posters since their entries were made, but I have respected their privacy in these reprints. None of my critics, however, have ever "come out" publicly one way or another.

Edits have been made to these posts, mostly for grammatical reasons or when certain tangents veered away from the conversation. In all cases, I have endeavored to maintain the intent and tone of the posters. I begin with some of the earliest responses to my article and follow-up letters to the editor that began after my announcement of the talk I'd be giving.

One more clarification for the reader: In lengthier posts, I've indicated paragraph breaks with three asterisks *** to save space.

The 1ˢᵗ Thread

heamme It plainly states in Leviticus 18 verse 22 "Do not lie with a man as one lies with a woman, that is detestable." This is when God is speaking to Moses and he tells him to go tell the Israelites. God wanted them to live as forgiven people. If you read all of Chapter 18 it is very matter of fact in what God expects of us to live a life pleasing to Him. I will continue to pray for all those who choose to live against God! I do not hate! I just think that society has accepted an unacceptable practice and therefore God's truth has been clouded. Read the Bible. It is amazing!

skepto Dude, that's the Old Testament. The one that also says that haircuts will send you downstairs. The one that says that an uncircumcised boy is to be abandoned by his parents and community. The one where if you're not Jewish, you're screwed. The one where interracial couples are bad. The one where a guy lives in a whale. Remember those parts too? What protection do you have from that God? I sure hope that you're kosher too...

blue ac I so agree with you! Skepto... If you want to live by the Bible, then you do not pick and choose which parts you do not want to believe or distort what is written. Are you continuing to get haircuts? Have you had any pork? Judge not lest ye be judged.

skepto If you don't approve in gay relationships, don't get into one. Beyond that, I'm not sure how it is really anyone else's business.

pistol pete It's our business when you try to force your values upon us...See, this is when it's my business as well, the NT is full of Condemnation of homosexuality (not repentant homosexuals).

skepto Forcing their values on you!?!?!?!!? YOU are FORCING your values on THEM! Find it in the Gospel. Get the big JC on record hating gays. It's not there without some really flexible interpretations...

pp At least I can admit I am wrong for doing the things that I do. I do not distort the written word in the Bible to suit my needs the way some do so that they will feel comforted in their sins.

goodfella Tony, as a Christian, I am greatly offended with your article. When someone is to write an article to the newspaper, it is usually a good idea to have researched the topic on which you are talking, and for you to be as ignorant as to say that the Bible has nothing in it that condemns homosexuals, is mind blowing, because Leviticus 20:13 absolutely does say that to be gay is wrong, and if you are to misinterpret something that couldn't be more straightforward in its meaning, it certainly makes someone question your credibility. Though you do have your freedom of speech, which means you can freely talk about your point of view on this, but it will and should greatly offend any Christian. All we, as Christians, can do is pray for you and hope that you can learn a little more about God and his book.

pp Jesus IS Judgment... And for you "Judge not" babblers...OK, I will judge me: It is wrong for me to murder. Judge for yourself if it's wrong for anyone else...It is wrong for me to violate the Order of God, Stated here by Jesus: *"And he answered and said unto them, Have ye not read, that he which made them at the beginning made them male and female, And said, For this cause shall a man leave father and mother, and shall cleave to his wife: and they twain shall be one flesh?"* *** No other Plan. No other examples of any other Arrangement. The bottom line to all! We all must follow God's laws and He will do the judging. I, as a Christian, have faith that the Bible is God's law and I will not dispute any of the teachings in it. I feel that society today does not want to sacrifice their "freedoms" to God's law, so they hide behind its validation or twist and turn its verses to suit their lifestyle. That is the devil working or do you not believe in him either? *** You have all the homosexual relationships you wanna, but it is wrong of anyone to try to force me to think it is OK when I don't...

puddy tat Tony's letter is disgusting.

pp The Greek text used to establish the Bible are FIVE THOUSAND DOCUMENTS SPANNING TWO THOUSAND YEARS AND ARE, AS JESUS SAID, EXACT COPIES DOWN TO THE DOTTING OF AN "I" AND THE CROSSING OF A "T". Now, if you have over five thousand documents exactly the same over thousands of years, that is MIRACULOUS!!! 'Sides, I have communicated with the Author. He's still of the same Opinion as when He had those others write it down... *** The argument that y'all have tried to "bait and switch" out of is this: Does the Bible condemn homosexuality as a sin? The answer, simply put is: YES... *** End of discussion....

You are close when citing the number of surviving Biblical manuscripts (either as fragments or whole texts of particular books) as being about 5,000 [actually closer to 5,500], but you are totally in error claiming there are no discrepancies among them. Biblical scholars have noted that there are more differences among those documents than there are words in the entire New Testament.

pp Yawn...Yawn again...Nothing new here. Not even a clear understanding of the tired and old...

debbie diamond Tony is a trouble maker. I have relatives who are gay, and have worked with gay people; no problems! I do not care what they do in the bed room, as others who have said, GOD will judge us all according to our sins. Let them MARRY if that makes them happy, does not affect me one way or another. We all have an opinion! There are more important issues at this time.

I find it interesting that my letter has generated such a variety of responses. When this leads to constructive dialogue, it's to be applauded. Unfortunately, a number of responses, on both sides of the issue, seem to be a bit confrontational. The purpose of my talk is to engender dialogue, and I hope that everyone who has posted will feel welcome to come and participate. I would like to point out that many of the statements that have been made concerning Scripture are addressed in my talk, and even though many believe that they are reading condemnations of homosexuality in the Bible, I maintain that nothing could be further from the truth. This forum is hardly the best venue for exchanging insights, but I have high hopes that everyone who feels they have something to contribute will be able to attend.

dd No, Mr. Marconi, I won't give you the satisfaction of my attendance at your bizarre talk. God vs. Gays?......guess who wins?

pp Y'all attend your "freakers' ball" and all, just don't hope your lies about what is and isn't in the Bible will stand... *** God Can and Will Forgive every kind of sin, including homosexuality. One must first repent. That is the Bible...And t, you know exactly what to expect seeing as you have done this many times before... *** 1 Corinthians 6:9 *"Know ye not that the unrighteous shall not inherit the kingdom of God? Be not deceived : neither fornicators, nor idolaters, nor adulterers, nor effeminate, nor abusers of themselves with mankind, 10 Nor thieves, nor covetous, nor drunkards, nor revilers, nor extortioners, shall inherit the kingdom of God. 11 And such were some of you: but ye are washed, but ye are sanctified, but ye are justified in the name of the Lord Jesus, and by the Spirit of our God."* *** Choose the Bible or choose t, not both... (gasp) What??? Is that the word "choose"??? (gasp again) If you simply look for those who will support your sexual anomaly, you will find it at the "lecture". If you seek the Word of God, I say to get it from God Himself and then you won't have to worry...

ditto Replying to pp: Know also that if you do not agree with t, you will be "uninvited" to share... ;-)

Not true—your input will be welcome, pp (you, too ditto)—If you choose to attend. It would be nice, in the meantime, if this forum would be used for something other than creating straw-man arguments and accusations. And by the way, your quotes from Corinthians and Mark are out of context and do not refer to homosexual orientation. But that's the reason I am giving this talk—to try to shed some light on those "clobber verses" that have too long been used to batter our LGBT brethren. Hope to see you tonight.

pp The context is obvious...Just because you "sell" your views to people desperate to buy doesn't make it a good product...I won't attend because the Mercy and Forgiveness of God will be tread underfoot. I will pray for each and every person in attendance though! *** I will not open my mind or my heart to falsehood. I won't comment on Tony's intentions though I know them. His "research" and the conclusions he draws from them are pitiable attempts to justify the behavior of a loved one. It isn't a matter of a closed mind, it's a matter of one that works well enough to assess the true value of what he preaches and find that value to be zero. No malice. No hatred. Only disinterested logic that renders his conclusions unsupported...

Professing to know the heart and intentions of another goes way beyond disinterested logic and unsupported conclusions. *** I am disappointed that a number of critics seem bent on arguing with what they think I have to say but chose not to attend my talk and hear what I actually said. Their criticisms might be more valid if only they'd take time to know what it is they are actually criticizing. I am sure it is not their intent, but whether they realize it or not, their often strident and doctrinaire rhetoric creates a perception of bullying to LGBT people. I doubt that this is the message they want to project, and yet there it is. If one considers the Bible to be the Word of God, then it strikes me that it would probably be desirable if we actually understand the Hebrew and Greek words used in the texts and to comprehend the mindsets of the men who wrote them. That is the topic I speak on, and I would be more than happy to sit with any individual who would like to engage in a truly meaningful dialogue on this subject.

    pp I know the Greek and the Hebrew. I know what you teach. What you teach is false. I know Tony's motives since he told them to me before and I see they haven't changed. I attended a prior lecture and was told that this one has nothing new to offer...I'm only responsible for what I say and do. God Knows my heart. I'm not responsible for those who seek out offense whether any is intended or not...

    Please enlighten me, pp: If I've told you my motives, what did I say they were? If you've attended one of my lectures, where was it, and what do you think the Hebrew and Greek say in Leviticus, Romans, and Corinthians? I can assure you, it's not what you claim when you take them out of context, using archaic English. And who told you my talk had nothing new to offer? Who are you, pp, that you claim to know me so well? I don't hide behind a post-name that allows me to take cheap shots at others or to claim I have exclusive insight as to what God thinks.

    pp Heh, heh, heh... getting under your skin, huh? I'm not hiding, I'm letting others decide whether what I say is truth on the merit of what is said.

    ringding Yes, pp, why don't you come out from behind your door and openly have a discussion with Tony? If you know so much of "God's book" and intentions, it would be easy for you to make mincemeat of Tony's reasoning and research. You rarely offer a logical or sound reason for most of your opinions, just that others are "wrong" but you are on the righteous side of the Lord. Everyone has an opinion—let's hear you debate your beliefs and opinions with Mr. Marconi, so we can all judge for ourselves. I think many of us would like to hear such a debate. Are you up for it?

pp My views are expressed and supported all over this and other forums. I see, t, and it seems, he knows that when I stop posting to this thread, there is nothing y'all can add...How about we do it that way? You have the opportunity to enlighten and instruct all us poor, hateful Christians by posting your "research and findings"...Please do so and let's all see if they stand the light of day...

Here you go:

Ehrman, Bart D., Lost Christianities, Oxford University Press, New York, 2003

Ehrman, Bart D., Misquoting Jesus, HarperSanFrancisco, 2005

Helminiak, Daniel A., What the Bible Really Says About Homosexuality, Alamo Sq. Press, 2000

Spong, John Shelby, Rescuing the Bible from Fundamentalism: A Bishop Rethinks the Meaning of Scripture, Harper San Francisco, 1992

Spong, John Shelby, The Sins of Scripture, HarperSanFrancisco, 2005

White, Mel, What the Bible Says — and Doesn't Say — About Homosexuality, Soulforce Inc, Lynchburg, VA, www.soulforce.org (24 pp., undated)

Wilson, Glenn, and Qazi Rahman, Born Gay: The Psychobiology of Sex Orientation, Peter Owen Publishers, 2005

pp heh, heh, heh...

Sorry, pp—I thought I was speaking to an adult. If your purpose of posting was to get under some of your readers' skins, then you might have had the decency to let us know you were only playing childish "gotcha" games from the beginning. Your responses have become defensive non- sequiturs, and there is no way to engage constructively with them. They are dialogue killers. If that is what you mean to happen, congratulations: You've triumphed.

goodfella Well, I'm coming late to the party but...I agree. I wish people would go back and read what you wrote. It's stated very well. Had to go through a lot of muck and mire dialogue to get there but finally did. *** Tony , I think what made the whole "I want honest and constructive dialogue" thing fall apart for you is coming out of the gate and saying something as ignorant as the Bible says nothing to condemn homosexuality. If you believe that it is a matter of context, interpretation, culture and the like then say that. Say others see it different than you and you are interested in hearing different beliefs in a conversation. But you came out with a wall and got met with walls. That's not a big shocker. I personally believe the Scripture does say homosexual sex is a sin the same as many other sins. I also believe the church in some areas has done a lousy job reaching out to, loving, and communicating with the GLBT community. I think the "us" versus "them" mentality shown in the comments on this thread testifies to that as well and grieves me.

Actually, I did make the point that what the Bible has to say is a matter of context, interpretation, and culture, and that by going beyond archaic English translations of the texts, those factors would negate the traditional arguments that define homosexuality as a sin. I stand ready to make my case. My letter stated fact, but I did welcome dissenting, civil dialogue from any who disagreed with me. That is not a wall; it is an open door— one that, so far, none of the responders on this site have chosen to walk through. This saddens me. Continuing to make the claim

that Scripture condemns gays without trying to understand what is really written in the Bible and what it actually means only perpetuates the social, spiritual, and often physical violence that victimizes LGBT people. I should think that all Christians would welcome the opportunity to correct these injustices.

gf I see what you are trying to say about your post, but I have to admit I think it's more your view of what you wrote than what you actually wrote. Some here have butted heads with you because they feel strongly and like to butt heads but not everyone. The fact that (as you state) no one has taken up a dialogue with you should hint to you that your intent versus what actually was put out there might not be the same. Just a thought. Listen, this is not a topic I have studied or address lightly. I have spent a ton of time studying the Bible from all the vantage points and simply cannot agree with you. I spent a week at the Emergent Summer Institute (before I knew what Emergent was) and spent at least 30 hours talking with Nanette Sawyer, Doug Paggit and others on this topic. I have spent 2 years talking about it on the Revolution NYC boards. I have straight friends on both sides of the topic, gay friends who believe it's ok, and gay friends who think it's not and are celibate. Some think I'm right, others think I'm a loving bigot. In other words, this is not a casual belief nor passing political topic for me. I believe the Bible is clear on the topic and while I have heard every defense for each passage, they don't hold enough water.

dd I like the title of your seminar, too. God vs. Gays...sounds like a war or a boxing match. I'm placing my bets on the big guy! I'm sorry, Tony, that the rest of us Christians disappoint you in our unwillingness to agree with you... Not really, I'm only worried about disappointing God and not man. You sir, are merely a man. Stop wagging your finger at us and calling us bigots, and take a look at your own life. Go back, get some more knowledge from God and please come back and tell us our faith is wrong! Please tell us how to correct it! PLEASE... I'm kidding, of course, I choose to get my enlightenment from God, not a flawed human being!

Actually, gf and dd, I did not call anyone a bigot. The implication was just the opposite—that decent Christians would not want to inflict pain on others but that many do so unintentionally. The title of my talk is "God vs. Gays: The War That NEVER Was." Taking my words out of context and reading personal insults into partial phrases used in identifying a serious problem in our civil and faith communities won't allow us to live in harmony with each other. I believe that the main point of Jesus' ministry was to encourage us to do exactly that.

dd Tony, I was pointing out, that I don't think you are what you are trying to profess to be...that's all. What do I perceive you are professing...that you want to unite everyone, just want us to get along. That's as long as we agree with you. What did I take out of context? I took the words from YOUR letter to the editor... Just my perception, I guess. *** Tony, I would never isolate or insult anyone, for any reason. That doesn't mean I agree with their lifestyle. *** Tony, I do have a theological question for you... Transgendered persons believe that a mistake was made before their births and they were "assigned" the wrong sex. Gays believe they were born that way, so God made them that way. Didn't God then also make the transgendered person the way they are before birth? In my "perception" transgendered people are saying God made a mistake, physically with them. It is my conviction God doesn't make mistakes...what about you?

gf I have a different perspective than God made people mentally challenged, physically challenged, gay, sick, transgender, etc... God set up creation and a process for us to multiply. It was never his original goal for any of these things to be a challenge in our lives. Once mankind rebelled... illness, sin, and hardship was introduced. We corrupted the original design. Just because we are born a certain way does not equal God made me this way. *** dd, I believe that transgender is not a mistake of God. I believe it's because the design of our procreation is corrupted due to sin being introduced. If there was no sin introduced, I don't believe there would be transgender folks, kids with cerebral palsy, or sin struggles.

    I agree—God doesn't make mistakes. I know a great many transgender people, some are like family to me. I've never heard one of them blame God for being who they are. They tend to use the word "mistake" as a reference to developmental processes. The religious transgender people that I know tend to think that God made them who they are and ask only to be respected for their desire to live as they honestly believe they were created to be. Genitalia alone do not define gender. Witness intersexed persons (both sets of genitalia) and those who physically present as women but have XXY chromosomes and cannot conceive. Same sex behaviors and pair bondings occur in over 300 vertebrate species, and heterosexual parents produce homosexual children in about 1 in 20 births. While there is no evidence of any socio-cultural causation of homosexuality, there is mounting scientific evidence that it is genetic/hormonal processes *in uteri* that determine orientation.

    pp My, my, my...There are no "transgendered" people, there are only mutilated males and females...Homosexuality is a choice...God doesn't Make mistakes...The issue is never sin, but is and always has been Forgiveness...If you wish to denounce the Bible, denounce it all and quit saying you are "Christian"...

    gf Here's the rub though: If you agree with me with transgender then the line "It's ok that I'm gay because God made me that way." goes out the window. (Not saying Tony said this but have heard from other areas). If we agree that that you can be born gay but that does not mean God made you that way... then there is ample reason to believe that it is part of being born into a corrupt and sinful world just like other sexual and intimacy desires.

I know that a lot of people consider homosexuality to be "unnatural," but I think that the growing body of neurobiological research is leading us to the opposite conclusion. I don't think this contradicts Scripture in any way. The Bible has at least 2 references in Leviticus, 1 in Romans, and 2 words in Corinthians (one repeated in 1 Timothy) that show definite disapproval for same sex acts that are based in lust by heterosexuals (Romans), prostitution (Corinthians), and non-procreative sex by Jewish males during the Babylonian Captivity (Leviticus). But I don't think we can define sexual orientation (either gay or straight) by non-procreation, lust, and prostitution. I believe that the Bible is concerned about the misuse of our sexual capacity rather than orientation as we understand it today. *** It's knowing what my LGBT friends have been put through—are being put through all too often—that motivates me to action. What I'm hoping to do in this life is to raise awareness that our LGBT brothers and sisters are regular recipients of such negatives, not so much made by malicious people but by decent people who don't realize the damage they are inadvertently inflicting. Whenever I hear someone saying that they are criticizing gays out of love, I have to go with Kurt Vonnegut's observation of such expressions of concern: "Please, a little less love and a lot more common decency." If we believe God loves everyone, we don't need to bang anyone over the head with a few Biblical verses to get that message across. We can do it by being inclusive and welcoming in our communities and by modeling that love in our daily lives.

dd Tony, I'm not mean! I would never isolate or insult anyone based on sexuality, race, etc. Just because I don't believe in a lifestyle, doesn't mean I'm hateful. I will continue to teach my children, homosexuality IS a sin, but we hate or judge no one. I wouldn't dare to begin to judge anyone else, I have enough issues of my own! :) I was truly curious about the transgendered thing. Thanks to all who added their input! I still don't get it though! If it is "genetic" wouldn't we see this anomaly in more people? Wouldn't it trend in certain groups, as most diseases do?

gf If we agree that sin affected procreation (our DNA makeup) then what doctors and scientist found would agree with and support that. *** Having several different reasons to explain away several different references in the Scripture has always seemed suspect to me. Like a defense attorney trying multiple things trying to find a reasonable doubt to win the case.

dd Gf, I agree with you. I'm saying if this WERE genetic, we would have proof of it. I don't believe it is (transgender or homosexuality), therefore they are not born that way. By saying they were (the transgendered) given the wrong sex at birth, I believe they are saying God isn't perfect and makes mistakes! How can one truly revere and worship a less than perfect God? *** Gf, I'm going to get ripped apart for this one, but... I believe it is an unclean spirit that causes homosexuality. I don't believe people are born to be murderers, rapists, etc., just like I don't believe God allows people to be born gay. Why would God say it is a sin, and then allow you to be born with that particular disposition to that sin??

gf They might rip you but I don't. We can have different thoughts without ripping each other. I do believe in evil and Heavenly principalities and their interaction in our lives. It's an interesting thought.

dd Could you agree then, gf, that God would not predispose us to abominable acts? That is why I don't believe God creates gay people. If we agree the Old Testament is relevant, then homosexuality IS an abomination before God. Since I believe people are not born gay, I believe they can be delivered and forgiven of their sins.

pp We will see repentant homosexuals, right along with the repentant adulterers, fornicators... See, this is what has been missing from this whole "discussion". The *fact that God not only*

*Can, but Will, Forgive ANY AND EVERY SIN of those who obey Him...*Like I said, the focus of this exchange has been about sin, rather than about the God Who Forgives sins...The stated "target" was Christians, was it not? Just whose doctrine has it promoted?

I do believe this forum is really too limited for serious discussions of theology. We all see ourselves as people of faith and as Christians, but our Christologies are radically different. That's to be respected and even encouraged. But the problem with trying to define God and Christ as we experience Them requires, for me at least, too much background content to convey it without the kind of Q & A that a good face-to-face dialogue can produce. I've given sermons on this topic before, and the conversations with my fellow parishioners afterwards were lengthy (and still ongoing).

pp This issue isn't at all complicated. It simply comes down to this and this alone: God Established marriage as being between a male and a female. There is no other Sanctioned set up. Homosexual "relations" are outside of His Model, and are therefore, sin. Amazing how complicated folks try to make this. Ask yourselves, is that for God's Reasons or for your own motives...

dd Why can't we say homosexuality is a sin and not be homophobic? I am not fearful of gays, I don't hate them. I would honestly say it's not my business who you choose to bed. I will tell my children God thinks it's a sin, just like lying, stealing, etc. Does that make me criminal-phobic because I think those things are wrong as well? I don't search out thieves and persecute them because they sin, just like I don't gays. I do say...don't live your life like them, the Bible says Jesus doesn't approve.

pp God in Jesus Christ, when asked about marriage and divorce Said: Matthew 19:4... *What therefore God hath joined together, let not man put asunder...* No other Model. So, since marriage is between a male and a female, homosexual acts are outside of marriage and therefore, fornication. Fornication is a sin. Homosexuality is a sin. Anything else I can help you with? He was asked about divorce. He Answered by defining marriage. By Defining marriage, He Told the Pharisees that there is no divorce granted by any man. *** There's this thing called "Accam's [sic] razor". It goes kinda like this: If you're in a rodeo and you hear hoof beats, think horse and not zebra. When applied to the verse in question, one then thinks marriage/divorce is the topic of both the question and the answer. In fact, since Defining marriage would also Answer the question of the Pharisees, this verse is not the hoof beats but indeed, the horse itself...Put another way, you REALLY gotta reach way beyond any reason to make this into anything else...There is only one sin: To put your will above the Will of God.

Jesus was speaking on the permanency of marriage. The problem with quoting Jesus quoting Genesis out of context is twofold. First, Matthew 19:4-5 simply records Jesus' response to a specific question.

³ The Pharisees also came unto him, tempting him, and saying unto him, Is it lawful for a man to put away his wife for every cause?

After answering, he is asked to defend his answer. Continuing with verses 7-9, it is clear that Jesus is defining marriage as it was traditionally given in Jewish culture, *only as a clarification of when divorce is permitted*. He was not asked to define all marriage for all time, especially since the patriarchs often practiced polygamy. Besides, several other forms of Old Testament marriage were still in effect in Jesus' day, not the least of which was Levirate marriage which required a childless widow to leave her home, marry her brother-in-law, and bear a child which was then considered to be sired by her deceased husband.

Jesus' follow up message was given thus:

⁷ "Why then," they asked, "did Moses command that a man give his wife a certificate of divorce and send her away?"

⁸ Jesus replied, "Moses permitted you to divorce your wives because your hearts were hard. But it was not this way from the beginning. ⁹ I tell you that anyone who *divorces his wife, except for sexual immorality, and marries another woman commits adultery, and whoever marries a divorced woman commits adultery.*

That was it. No absolutist remarks about there being only one kind of marriage, since He was not asked that question.

The second problem with your argument, pp, is that in assuming that because the first two prototype humans were a male and female, all love relationships were supposed to be heterosexual. But nowhere in Genesis is this stated. Such an assumption is an argument framed in the negative and impossible to prove. And yet, there are many more things left out of the story than are given. What were Adam and Eve's race, eye and hair color, etc. To have over six billion permutations off that original pair, then they must have contained the countless genetic-hormonal combos to begin with. Sexual orientation is only one of these. *** I understand why it is so important to the traditional arguments against homosexuality that this orientation be considered a choice. If one were to accept—as science now indicates—that it is a minority expression of developmental processes occurring *in utero*, then arguing for it being "wrong" implies an unwillingness to accept God's plan for creation. Ascribing homosexuality to the Fall would be one way to avoid this contradiction, but one would have to find clear statements in the Bible that it is a sin. This is never stated. The lists of references given in other posts are based on biases about homosexuality brought to the readings by those arguing in the negative. The Hebrew and Greek do not support them. Only using translations of the Scriptures based on the English idiom of

Shakespeare's day are such references defensible. Pp, your zeal notwithstanding, you are not the final arbiter of God's word—especially when you patch it together outside of its linguistic and cultural contexts.

dd It's wrong to say homosexuality is a sin, but it's ok to say Christians make virtues out of not thinking??? Never once have I discriminated against ANYONE for ANY reason, yet I have been name called, and they attempt to belittle and insult at every turn. Point out my "bias" while ignoring their own towards those who disagree with them. You can stand against something in a peaceful, loving way! Contrary to the behavior I see here, you can disagree and not call names, discriminate against, or hate. Try it sometime...

pp Love 'em all ya want. Just don't have sex with them! What's it to you anyway? You certainly aren't Christian...The "problem" isn't that people hate Christians or the Bible and such. The "problem" is someone saying the Bible says things it simply does not. Argue all the other stuff *ad nauseum*, but the Word is the Word...This entire topic was spawned by one man's attempt to bring condemnation and contempt upon Christians...You can read, can you not?

I have attempted to speak as a Christian to other Christians. Not once have I condemned or shown contempt for other Christians who disagree with my approach to Scriptures. Pp, I don't dispute—never have disputed—your right to believe as you see fit. But I said it before, and I'll say it again: It is one thing to say you believe that God thinks this or God wants that, but it's entirely another to make the claim that you speak for God. If anyone is showing contempt for the Christian faith, it is you who claims to be the arbiter of God's will. If that's your notion of Christ's message, it's no wonder Jesus wept. *** I'm hoping to make this clear, dd: At no time did I call you a bigot or question the validity of your beliefs or refer to you as a homophobe. I did not and do not claim to speak for God. But because I refer to the heterosexism that is rampant in our society, you seem to conclude that I was attacking your faith. What I said was that we all bring biases to the reading of Scripture. This is true of every one of us as we approach everything in life. We are always going to see issues through the frames we've developed from our own life experiences. But please don't suppose I consider you a bigot or homophobic or that your Christology is wrong just because it is different than mine. I responded to these posts, from the beginning, in the spirit of encouraging respectful dialogue. This will be an impossibility if every criticism of a theological question is treated as a personal attack or insult. None are intended, I respect our differences. *** Gf, I think I need to clarify something you think I said or that I said awkwardly. I don't believe that homosexuality was caused by the Fall. My thesis is this: If one claims that homosexuality was caused by the Fall, then one must either conclude that heterosexuality is also a sin or one must find specific sources in Scripture that single out homosexuality specifically as a sin. If such a citation exits, I only ask to be told where it is. As I've mentioned several times now, the five or six specific citations usually tossed out do not refer to orientation but to specific same sex acts that are disapproved of. The misuse of sex—not orientation itself—is what is condemned or disparaged, depending on which verses one examines. *** I'll offer one example of what I mean about how our biases can impact on our interpretations of the Biblical texts: The story of Sodom. Traditionally, it is said that God destroyed Sodom because of the attempted rape of two angels disguised as men. The men of Sodom turned down Lot's daughters, so it assumed they must have been gay and their act was the straw that broke the camel's back as far as God was concerned. But rape is a crime of brutality in which sex is used as the weapon, and it was understood that way in Lot's day as well. It was routinely employed as one of an arsenal of tools that would "encourage" strangers to "get out of Dodge." Strangers could be trouble and had to be vetted by the town's elders—something the Sodomites claimed Lot failed to do. Lot's daughters were valuable property as long as they remained intact. Raping them would be tantamount to starting a lot of internal struggle, not to mention comprising an act of theft and destruction of property. Besides, they were not relevant to the issue at hand: getting rid of the strangers. The same mindset seems to be at work in Judges 18 in the town of Gibeah, where an almost identical attack occurs. The actual rape that was committed there was heterosexual in nature, but this isn't a condemnation of straights. The six Bible writers who cite the actual sins of Sodom are Ezekiel 16:48-49, Wisdom 9:13, Matthew (quoting Jesus) 10:11-15, Isaiah 1:10 and 3:9, Jeremiah 23:14, and Zephaniah 2:8-11. The first three cite violations of hospitality codes, and the last three list injustice, oppression, partiality, adultery, lies, and encouraging evil doers. None of them list same-sex activities as one of the city's sins. A person of faith can speculate as to the nature of other sins perpetrated in Sodom. But that's not the word of God. It's human speculation. If one has a "gay equals sin" bias, then that's what one will conclude, but the Bible never says it. Not there, not anywhere. Civil comments welcome.

gf My final on the GLBT issues as I think at this point we are all going in circles. Tony and I have similar views on a couple of the verses he refers to and very different views on some others. I still think the best exploration for anyone who will actually click a link and read is *http://www.gaychristian.net/greatdebate.php* by two men who are vested in this topic. *** Besides that, time for a break from the current cycle of the topic. Thanks guys for the conversation....

Pp, you have the right to be respected for your opinions, but if others disagree, it does not make them anti-Christian, anti-God, or even anti-you. The zeal of your faith is duly noted and accepted. But the virulence that it is sometimes cloaked in often makes dialogue with you difficult. I'd like to engage with reason and civility. *** The fact that so many exchanges have occurred on these pages tells me that there is a need to air out a lot of diverse opinions on this subject. That is what my talk was designed to do, and that is more or less what happened here, although without most of the people who commented actually hearing what they were commenting about in the first place. I have delivered my talk over the past several years to hundreds of people, and an amazing range of divergent perspectives have been expressed among the varied participants. Some of the attendees have been non-religious, some extremely religiously conservative. Most have been somewhere in the middle. All showed each other respect, and many from both sides of the issue have thanked me for supplying the forum. No one has ever said they felt insulted or marginalized. Unfortunately, this forum tends to encourage anonymous expressions of anger toward "straw men" or other misperceived enemies. Anyone care to have a nice face-to-face chat?

pp We proved you dead wrong...The readers who are honest need only ask who has offered their opinions in simple, straightforward manners and who has twisted and turned and pounded the meaning of words into the shapes they molded for them from the beginning...Yes, yes, heap the condemnation upon me...Heap it upon us all...We have the audacity to disagree... *** You have done NOTHING to change what Jesus Said and Meant Not...One...Thing...All you posted is why you feel secure in NOT BELIEVING WHAT IS PLAINLY WRITTEN IN BLACK AND WHITE...It's pitiful...Oh snap! I knew it! Middle-earth and Frodo Baggins really did exist! Fairy tales.... *** Let's let t have one last lick? This ground has been plowed and plowed and plowed... *** There is nothing to discuss. That's been my point all along. You are obviously incorrect in almost all of your assertions. The one verse that I posted proves this beyond any further argument or discussion. Since there is nothing to discuss, I do not discuss it. The truth is the truth and I tell it as the truth. I have done EXTENSIVE research and poured over literally, every word in the New Testament and most of the Old Testament. My frustration is that I must compress hours and hours and hours' worth of research and supporting evidence into a coupla hundred words. And...However you want to put it, there are some real IDIOTS on here and I get caught up in defending myself OFTEN.

    Replying to pp's quote: "There is nothing to discuss...The one verse that I posted Proves this beyond any further argument or discussion."
I responded to that one verse explanation showing the context of the quote by Jesus. I tried to use reason to explain the actual point being made by Jesus. It had nothing to do with establishing a Divine prescription of marriage, but rather establishing the permanency of marriage under Jewish law in the 1st Century CE. Using a few sentences removed from the point Jesus was making about divorce to "prove" that God considers homosexuality a sin misrepresents and distorts Jesus' actual teaching. *** Let me point out that I have yet to have anyone respond to the arguments I've made about Sodom. I doubt anyone will at this point. In a way, it's a shame, because the opportunity for constructive dialogue seems to have been lost. We could have looked at Leviticus, Romans, and Corinthians and really examined what the P-writer and Paul were actually trying to say. Instead, I've been refused a reasoned response by anyone out there. And yet, my talks are usually well attended, and I keep getting positive feedback from the conservative Christians who attend them. Why the lack of desire to engage on these pages, do you suppose? Sadly, I am left with the impression that the few who have continued this post aren't interested in exchanging ideas and information on this subject. And yet, by refusing to open up to the possibility that there might be more to learn, you deny yourselves the opportunity to teach (not preach to) others. I'm sorry for both our losses. *** I have had to respond to accusations from pp about my supposed hidden agenda to denigrate Christians and attack their faith. I have repeatedly stated that I also am a Christian, but apparently my Christology isn't one that is respected on these pages. Most posters have labeled me "Ignorant" or have accused me of calling them names

or implying they are bigots because I've chosen to state an obvious truth: Heterosexism is rampant, harmful, and often inadvertently perpetrated by people of faith who would not intentionally harm others if they knew they were doing it. *** Throughout these exchanges with pp and others, I have tried to state verifiable facts about those Bible verses so many Christians use to claim that God disapproves of gays. I've attempted to discuss these passages reasonably. *** I think religion can be an incredible force for good as well as one used to perpetrate evil. Human beings are fallible, and the road to Hell is often paved with good intentions. I believe that if people of good faith try to behave ethically, whether they follow the teachings of Jesus, Mohammad, Buddha, Confucius, etc., they will find their connection to that Process I call God. (You might prefer the Force, just to keep it secular.) I find my connect through Jesus, but others do it through a variety of ways. One doesn't need to believe in God to be ethical, but I am wary of those who tell me they speak the only truth FOR God. I am a religious (and social) liberal, but my understanding of Jesus sees Him as one, too. Others will disagree, but I have expressed from the start that I respect those differences between us. *Pax vobiscum.*

    pp I'd rather someone hate me and walk away having at least heard the truth than love me and not hear it. *** I know what I mean when I write this stuff, so you jigs are actually rather amusing to me... T, t, t, t...You are an EXPERT at what I haven't said, what Paul and those who penned the Bible haven't said and what God hasn't said...you wouldn't last twenty seconds with me in a cage match, once I got 'hold of you...In the end and the End, all that will matter to me is what God Thinks about me. If you have a problem with me, take it up with Him. To that end, did you pray as I asked you? If so, what did God Tell you? Oh, and I ONLY WANT TO HEAR WHAT HE HAD TO SAY...If you didn't pray and/or didn't get an Answer, I will pray that your darkness no longer persists, God Willing!

liverite Tony, I completely disagree and find it dangerous that you say we can "choose" how we interpret the Scriptures. And sir, quite frankly, that's where you are just plain dangerous to the lives of others of what you're putting out there. God says what God says and we don't get to choose how we interpret it. What God says, is what God says for all in His Word. We find the truth, not define it. *** Also, Tony, you pledged your life work to be civil rights for the LGBT community. No choice, I'll disagree. I can choose to change my lifestyle if I desire. So could you. Some may feel they have no choice, but there is. It depends on if and what you choose to act upon. To say they're incapable to choose is an insult to their ability to determine their own feelings and who THEY love. Right/wrong is a view. So...If tomorrow, God says that being straight is a sin, you would have "no problem choosing" to be gay??

momzy Tony points out the hurt that "many Christians" unknowingly cause the LGBT community by using Scripture to condemn homosexuality. And as I am sure Tony has calculated, he gets the typical responses as seen here. Many different views and harsh remarks. Now momzy is more than willing to go toe to toe with Tony on the Scriptures he cites. In fact, momzy just might do that. *** I do want to say that there is a strong element of truth in what Tony says regarding behavior towards homosexuals. Even in the most respectable Christian denominations, many times homosexuals are laughed at and made fun of. And it may very well hold true that homosexuals are predisposed to be this way. You see, because of the human condition, we all have this hang up as to which of us are better! We all have this code of Christian' ethics and give each sin a certain score as to which is the worst. Now we label certain sexual sins as way out there. While lying may be a 3 on the sin scale...the homosexuals...they usually get a 10. *** Then Tony comes along and says that it's not even on the 'sin' list. Thus, the vehement protest against the sin we usually give a '10' to. But I ask Tony again, as a Christian, without the homosexual issue, what would your message be? There is no trap here. Have I not described this issue with some accuracy?

Oh, I suppose I could find a couple of things to turn my efforts toward—poverty issues, environmental degradation, improving our educational system, etc. You know—the usual liberal stuff. For that matter, there's still a lot of racism, sexism, classism out there to go around. As a person of privilege and a person of faith, I believe I have an opportunity to connect with God by trying to extend the privileges I've been given to those who have not had the advantages I have. I've been working on LGBT rights almost exclusively for the past 7 or 8 years and will continue to do so until things change or I pass on. At this point, I think full civil rights for gays are less than 20 years away, so with a little luck, I'll be around to see it happen. *** Meantime, I want to note that no matter who is reading the Bible, we all bring our own perspectives to it. The inspired authors were responding to their experiences in their times and cultures. They didn't write in English. They often took positions we reject today, e.g., slavery, menstruating women, animal sacrifices, stoning certain sinners— even divorce. *** Time and circumstances often obscure their original meanings and if we don't attempt to understand the actual language they used and the cultural context in which they used it, then how can we claim to know the Word of God through them? *** I'm sure that the way we express our understanding of God is different, but I would never call your belief heretical. This implies that there is only one way to come to God and that all others are wrong. I was fed enough of that growing up pre-Vatican II Catholic. I rejected that notion then and I reject it even more now. But, that's just me.

pp I take issue with anyone claiming to be a Christian and then saying there are many paths to God when Christ was very clear on the topic. To be Christ like and then water Him down is heretical.

Take whatever issue you want, but it still does not authorize you to be God's spokesman. Meanwhile, let me try to move onto something more productive by examining a pair of the clobber verses that take many Christians down the wrong path and cause them to disparage gays in the name of their faith. Leviticus, Chapter 18:22 reads non-idiomatically in the Hebrew: "With a male, you shall not lie the lyings of a woman; it is an offense." 20:13 repeats the admonition for both participants in the act and adds the penalty of death for violation. Both passages were a part of the holiness code written for Jews being held captive in Babylon about 2600 years ago. The main purpose of the Law was to keep Jewish culture intact by defining the ways in which Jews were to conduct every aspect of their lives as separate from the Gentiles and in ritual covenant with God. *** The overarching concept behind the Law was the maintenance of cleanliness. For example, things that lived in the water should have scales and fins or they were unclean. Clean animals had cloven hooves and chewed the cud. Pigs had cloven hooves but didn't chew their cud and were therefore unclean. *** Nothing clean was to be mixed with something unclean (menstruating women were forbidden to even touch a man), and even clean things should not be mixed lest the combination result in something unclean being produced. Hence, you did not harness an ox and donkey together to plow. Only one kind of crop could be grown in a field. Clothing could only be made of one kind of fiber. Dairy and meat could not be served on the same plate, and two men could not have penetrative sex with each other. In Hebrew, the word for woman is *naqeba* which means orifice-bearer. The lyings of a woman were receptive, of a man penetrative. If a man lay the lyings of a woman, he would be mixing his penetrative capacity with a female's receptive role. Because women were incapable of this "mixing of kinds," their "rubbings" (as the rabbinical scholars labeled their same-sex activities) were not punishable under Levitican law. *** The King James' version of the Bible calls this act an abomination, but the actual translation of the Hebrew word *to'eva* is simply "offense." When the Torah was translated into the Greek Septuagint (which were the texts Paul and Jesus would have used), to'eva is translated into *bdelygma,* meaning "a ritual offense." These kind of offenses would be forgiven after a series of ritual baths and prayers—even the death penalty would be put aside. Homosexuality is not limited or defined by two men not reproducing. If Leviticus was about condemning same-sex orientation, it would have included prohibitions for lesbians—which it clearly did not—and that issue was part of the Jewish oral tradition that became the Talmud and was specifically not condemned. Same sex behavior was not approved by the Jews, but their position had nothing to do with homosexuality—a concept that didn't even begin to be understood until about 150 years ago.

    gf While we each can interpret the Scripture differently, that doesn't mean we are all right, so I continue to reevaluate anything that people take different ways. To me, that is different than saying we can choose how we want to interpret Scripture.

    pp As for my impatience with some people, like t, it's because as I said, the nature and number of sins is irrelevant except to diagnose problems. The "danger" here is that someone might think they are not sinning when they really are and not seek Salvation...

    Replying to gf: Maybe we're getting hung up on semantics, gf. I finally finished reading both sides of your recommended post, and you seem to side with the celibate point of view expressed by Ron. I thought Justin made the better argument. The point is, we've both made choices which are reflective of the biases (predispositions toward a point of view) that we brought to the readings. I'm not saying your interpretation is wrong, but I don't believe any interpretation—yours, mine, (even pp's) are absolute. For me to accept the claim that there is only one unequivocally correct interpretation of Scripture or only one way to connect to God would leave no room for my faith to evolve. I believe that faith is a living thing that, like all living things, must grow or die. Understanding how the Scriptures became cannon, the politics involved, causes me to continue exploring them for meaning. *** One other quick note on the debate articles. Ron was being more than a bit disingenuous on at least two occasions. First, he quoted Mel White out of context to make his point about the Bible's concern with human sexuality, and second, for all his two years studying Greek, he still chose to translate *arsenokoetae* as "practicing homosexuals." Ascribing this late, late 20th Century, post-emergent gay rights movement definition to Paul's mindset says more about Ron's state of mind than it does the Apostle's. Homosexuality, as it has come to be defined and understood by 21st Century moderns was an unknown concept in Paul's day. Male prostitution was not. Which is more likely that Paul was referencing? And unless lesbians don't count as homosexuals, again the absence of concern for their behaviors in I Corinthians 9:6 is one more indicator that Paul was citing the misuse of sexuality and not orientation. Good debate; yes. Definitive? Not by a long shot.

gf Tony, not interested in debating the discussion on the "Great Debate", just offered out to everyone without trying to put my twist on it so they can make up their own minds. I can pick apart the one I disagree with too but my goal is to respect others to make up their own minds instead of trying to steer them my way.

The 2nd Thread

Sometime later, after I published the letter inviting people to the annual town fair, pp posted: "Suppose they gave a lecture and nobody came?" implying that there had been no interest in my presentation so nobody would be interested in discussing LGBT civil rights at the fair. By then, a state ballot initiative had been passed, defining marriage as only existing between a man and a woman. My invitation began the 2nd thread on the same site and with many of the same posters plus some new ones. Over the previous few years, I had responded to several of my critics in the paper by explaining the terms they objected to when I described some of the attitudes they expressed in print. Those definitions are as follows:

Stereotype: a labeling of a person based on perceptions of the group to which the individual belongs.

Prejudice: a belief system which "pre-judges" an individual based on a stereotype.

Discrimination: uttered words or specific actions based on a prejudice.

—ism (—ist): discrimination backed by power, including, but not limited to: race, gender, age, sexual orientation, religious belief, etc.

—phobia (—phobic): an irrational fear of a person or a group based on prejudice.

Bigot: someone holding irrationally to a stereotype and practicing prejudice and/or discrimination.

These definitions resulted in a number of posters accusing me of name calling, and this carried over onto the new thread. I begin with the following post:

> Responding to pp: *"Suppose they gave a lecture and nobody came?"* Actually, the attendees responded well to the information they received. I was even thanked by a local minister who felt I was making valid points. Beyond that, the several hundred visitors to our booths [at various festivals and fairs] who come to learn more about LGBT issues and to discuss the realities of the non-condemnation of homosexuality by the Bible showed how incredibly inaccurate that *"Suppose..."* comment to be. *** There is a hunger for justice for our marginalized gay brethren out there, and it is finding its expression even in our own town. One day our children and grandchildren will look back at the actions and attitudes of today's heterosexists (those who believe being straight is somehow superior to being gay) and the homophobes (people who are frightened for whatever reason by homosexuality) and wonder at their ignorance and their discriminatory words and actions. They are, after all, no different than racists. Same mentality; different targets. *** What I don't get is why anyone would purposely choose to discriminate and make other people's lives more difficult than is necessary. Why is it so important to have a set of privileges that can be denied to others? I'm speaking of marriage rights, employment and housing rights, etc. The problem with our churches fostering the myth that the Bible condemns homosexuality is that the members of those churches cast their votes in civil elections based on that nonsensical mantra that being gay is a sin. This attitude is an insult to the very teachings of Jesus Christ, and all the huffed-up pontificating to the contrary, it makes a mockery of His life.

> **debbie diamond** Tony, you have a label for everyone. Homophobic, heterosexist (etc.)... What title do you ascribe to yourself??? Oh, wait I got it... JUDGE!

I'm not the one self-describing himself by screeching heterosexist or homophobic remarks. It's not judging to label something for what it is. Cow meat is beef. A person who is a follower of Jesus is a Christian. Anyone assuming that being gay is inferior to being straight is a heterosexist. If they have an unwarranted fear of homosexuality or homosexuals, they are homophobic. Those are simple definitions, not judgments. People identify themselves by their words and actions. Sorry, debbie, if you're taking any of this personally. It isn't directed at any one person in particular. But it is the reason why I've dedicated myself to this cause, and whether or not I'll live to see social justice done for LGBT people, I have the satisfaction of knowing that my work and volunteerism is contributing to its eventual triumph.

puddy tat The gay lifestyle is wrong and nothing you say will change that.

Lifestyle? Ah, yes. That would be holding a job, raising kids, keeping up with house and yard work, attending church, getting together with friends, being married or partnered or single and dating. Seems to me that lifestyle is about the same whether you're gay or straight. So, I think you aren't referring to lifestyle but rather to whom someone is sleeping with. So, I have to ask: What possible difference could it make to you who someone else has a sexual relationship with? You're acting like being gay poses a threat to you personally, but homosexual orientation isn't contagious, you know. It is a condition of birth, and those who insist it's a choice are ill informed and are usually seeking to reconcile their anti-gay biases with religious viewpoints that make little sense either.

dd SO...if one thinks homosexuality is a sin...we are homophobic or heterosexist in your eyes. Not believers in the Bible??? Oh, I forgot. We haven't reached enlightenment like you, and therefore, are unable to receive the Biblical revelations that you have. I'm not scared of gays, so I'm not homophobic. I don't think I'm superior because I'm straight. So, you're going to need a new label for me!!! You accept everyone, except people who disagree with you!!! That is astounding!! I accept EVERYONE REGARDLESS of their color, religion, sexual orientation, etc. But it doesn't mean I agree with every aspect of their lives...

Never said that believing homosexuality = sin makes anyone either heterosexist or homophobic—just that it has both those repercussions when applied to our civil culture. I am glad you are so accepting of everyone, but then again, I never said any of this was about you. You aren't the point of this thread. I don't define people—we all define ourselves, and the cause of LGBT rights is advancing quite well with or without your particular approval. Thanks for your interest.

Dd Yep, and your definition is apparent. Do as I say (accept EVERYONE regardless) not as I do (pass judgment on others). So, it is possible, in your world to think homosexuality is a sin and not be a "phobic" or an "ist" ??? Just curious. How many other phobia and ist labels do you have in that bag-o-tricks anyway??

One thing I am sure of: You are not homophobic. It's fine by me if you want to think being gay is a sin. But that MAY make you heterosexist (believing that being straight is superior in some way to being gay). So, I'll keep staffing festival and fair booths and advancing the cause of full equality for gays. I know you support same-sex marriage rights, but can't you see that the main opposition to that civil right comes from our churches? Until we change our attitudes there, the fight will continue to go on longer than it has to. Twenty years from now, when our teens and twenty-somethings start being politically involved, the battle will be won. *** The operative word is MAY, debbie. Depends on whether or not you think being heterosexual is also a sin that should impact on straight people's civil rights. I don't know if you do, nor do I care. As I said, this thread is not about you. And a label is not a judgment. I think you are capable of telling the difference. My value system tells me heterosexism and homophobia are harmful attitudes. Whether or not that is true for you is your own business. I have not heard homophobia from you, but I may have heard heterosexism. If I did, I didn't say there was something wrong with you for being that way. I did say that heterosexism is creating a second-class citizenship status for gays. That's fact, and since you say you treat everyone the same, it shouldn't bother you. *** Racism, sexism, classism, creedalism— just to name a few things I find reprehensible and cause me to ask: Why is opposing an —ism a problem for any thinking, caring human being? And what "bag of tricks" am I using, debbie? Reason? Knowledge? Open mindedness? Caring for a minority's rights? In your own words: *"I accept EVERYONE REGARDLESS of their color, religion, sexual orientation, etc. but it doesn't mean I agree with every aspect of their lives..."* I've not asked for agreement, just an end to discrimination.

    dd No, you have asked for acceptance Tony. I have no problem accepting gays!! I don't care who ANYONE has sex with (as long as they do it responsibly) and I don't discriminate against them either. Again, because I don't condemn them, doesn't mean I condone them, either!!

    I still don't get why my denouncing heterosexism and homophobia is a problem for you. I haven't labeled you either— have stated quite categorically that you aren't the object of this thread. Yet you persist on making this about you. You can condone or condemn what you want, but unless you are reading your name into my denouncement of bigotry, I can't get why my advocacy for gay rights bothers you so much.

    dd I was alluding to your list of people we shouldn't discriminate against. I noticed every day, God fearing, working, Christians wasn't on that list. I don't like the fact you see no middle ground. But I think being gay is a sin. Others do too. It doesn't mean we think they should be discriminated against or treated differently!! Regardless of what you post, it is the underlying theme I take from it. I know you are married, so do you consider yourself a heterosexist?? (just curious)

youme Folks...those of you that believe homosexuality is a sin...are spinning your wheels debating this point on this forum. Mr. Marconi's previous posts clearly show the liberal left agenda: "Agree with me because you are wrong." If we try to explain our point of view...we are bigots and haters. There is no tolerance from the liberals. Mr. Marconi's interpretation of Biblical condemnation of homosexuality is interesting indeed. Literally hundreds of Bible scholars are united on the Scripture in Romans, Chapter One...the Homosexual lifestyle is sin.

Literally hundreds of other Biblical scholars disagree, and your use of the word "lifestyle" when referring to same sex behaviors indicates a problem with your understanding of what is being denounced in Romans. Homosexual orientation is never mentioned in Scripture because it was an unknown concept to the people who wrote the Bible. It is the misuse of sexuality (rape, lust, prostitution, failure of Jewish men to procreate) that was considered sinful. To claim homosexuality is a sin based on what is clearly NOT in Scripture makes about as much sense as claiming being left handed is a sin. Our sexuality is a part of our nature that goes far beyond simple reproduction for human beings. It is through our sexual interactions that our bonding with another allows us to find completion of ourselves with another; that draws us into relationships of nurturing and cherishing that make us, in many respects, fully human. 1 in 20 human beings are oriented to find that fulfillment in same sex relationships. Science tells us that this is the result of genetic/hormonal processes that happen in the womb. It seems as much a part of God's creative plan as is the differentiation of eye, hair, and skin color along with the other tens of thousands of physical traits that have resulted in over 7 billion permutations of the original 2 prototypes He first put on this earth. Same sex behaviors and pair bondings are

found in over 300 vertebrate species, so unless God didn't design them that way, you've got a problem with His order of nature. By the way, where do the intersexed (people having both male and female genitalia) fit into the Biblical creation story? They had to come from somewhere, and just because Genesis doesn't mention them doesn't make them sinners. *** [Responding to dd]: I don't think God fearing, working Christians are being made the object of institutional discrimination or I would be opposing their oppression as well. But there is a Catch 22 in the line of argument that says people who discriminate in their churches are opposed to discrimination in matters of civil rights. There are some for whom that may be true, but too many others take the stance that voting for LGBT civil rights is voting for sin. That goes beyond belief and does constitute an act of bigotry. I am passionate about social justice in general and LGBT rights in particular. And, FYI, I'm very married and very straight. *** I just wanted to add one more thought here as a way of clarifying where I'm coming from. I understand that this is the civil rights issue I personally choose to focus on, and I don't believe that someone has to be involved in this particular struggle to prove they're not a "—phoebe or an —ist." My struggle is with those who openly declare and/or otherwise display their anti-gay biases and who advocate for the status quo when it comes to granting LGBT people their just rights as citizens of this nation. If I seem single-minded in this cause, it's because mostly I am. If the time comes when this is no longer an issue, and I am still alive, I'll probably devote myself as passionately and single-mindedly to some other necessary cause. God knows there's enough injustice to last us all several lifetimes. (Makes me glad I don't believe in reincarnation.)

dd Are transgendered people born that way, too? If so... you're saying God makes mistakes. It is my religious view point, He doesn't. But it could be that view point makes little sense to you, also. I personally don't want to believe in a fallible God!! If I did, I would believe in Greek mythology, not Christianity.

blue ac Transgendered people are exactly as God intended them, if God is indeed infallible.

pistol pete Ignore Tony, and he will very quickly go away...

I agree that God doesn't make mistakes. **Transgendered people are as God made them, but who they are is known to them and God. God also makes intersexed persons (having both sets of genitalia), xxy chromosome people who present as female but are sterile, people born with almost no identifying genitalia at all, and on and on. Why be hung up one way or another about one in twenty persons whom God made gay? To argue that since God made a male and female as the first two human prototypes (while ignoring all the genetic/hormonal combinations within them that have resulted in billions of currently living permutations) somehow proves that being gay (which is only one minority expression of those combinations) is wrong makes no sense. It is an argument framed in the negative and assumes that the person making the claim knows what God thinks.**

binky There are so many divisions among churches that it's hard for new Christians to know what is legitimate and what is not. This is just another attempt to confuse people. If it's not of God, then it is of Satan. If you look hard enough you can find someone who will side with your cause. Set up all the booths you want. True Christians follow Christ's teachings and do not distort the word. One thing that is clear to me as I read the Scriptures is that Homosexuality is indeed a sin. I am very comfortable in my faith and see this distortion of the truth as a work of evil. For anyone that cares and wonders what is true, read the Bible from beginning to end and pray about it. Don't take someone's word or opinion to be fact.

Binky, perhaps you'd be willing to tell me where, exactly, in Scripture, homosexuality is so defined. Let me save you a little

time by telling you that if you're going to refer to the story of Sodom, Leviticus 18:22 and 20:12, Romans 1:22-32, or I Corinthians 6:9-10, you're barking up the wrong tree. None of those verses is about homosexual orientation—merely the misuse of sexuality (attempted rape, failure of Jewish men to procreate, lust, and male prostitution). If those are your notions of how sexual orientation is defined—either gay or straight—your problem is in understanding the nature of sexual orientation in human beings, and it's no wonder you're confused about what the Bible is actually saying. As a Christian, you owe it to yourself to get better educated on this topic before you continue to cause your LGBT brethren more pain. Jesus taught us to be better than that. *** One of Christ's teachings is not to judge your brethren. I set up booths because of people who think their narrow-minded views of LGBT people are expressions of "true" Christianity when nothing could be farther from the truth. Reading the Bible without understanding it in its historic and linguistic contexts only enables one to use it as a club to hit people they don't like with. As you said, just taking someone's opinion for fact isn't a good idea. I can present facts to counter your opinions, if you'd care to engage.

pp If you ignore him, he really does go away...

In the last thread on this subject, pp, you gave a display of poor Bible scholarship, claimed you knew what God actually meant, quoted Jesus out of context, and said I was rewriting the Bible. You also said you'd attended one of my lectures (which you obviously haven't) but refused to name the venue. I'm not surprised you want me to go away. *** Our Gay-Straight Alliance booth will be at a nearby county's fair for the 7th year in a row. We've been in yet another close by county fair three years running as well. So far, we've spoken to literally thousands of supporters and maybe a couple of dozen naysayers. They are usually polite—I've only encountered 3 or 4 total who ranted.

Other fairgoers who hear them rant tell us afterward how ignorant they sound. Kind of like these threads.

dd See binky...your Christianity isn't as evolved as Tony's. Don't try to use Scripture to back your claims, because even though you have read it, you don't have the Tony Marconi's guide to true enlightenment reference appendix, and the King James version...well, it's just so old. Tony...do good Christians run around calling other people ignorant? I don't remember Jesus calling people idiots because they didn't agree with him. Do you have your own Bible or does the King James version suffice for you??

koop The simple truth on this subject should be that one day each person will come face to face with their maker, and it is then and only then that we will learn what God thinks of our conduct on earth. However, as I read these posts, it would appear that most believe that Tony's recent talk on "God vs. Gays" should have been titled "Gays vs. God."

Too many people say my neighbor is my neighbor, but if s/he is gay, they must not have the same civil rights and legal protections I have. When that inconsistency ceases to be, I'll leave the – ists and –phoebes alone. Until then, I will continue to speak out against their bigotry. *** I agree it is up to God to judge. So, then, why are so many "Christians" doing the judging for Him, contrary to what Jesus taught us to do? How does anyone think they are acting as a Christian by pronouncing homosexuality to automatically be a sin when the Bible does not support that view. A person's perceived state of grace should never be the basis for granting them civil rights. Yet, that is exactly what these judgmental "Christians" do when they vote against civil marriage. *** Ignorance is lack of knowledge, not idiocy. Stating a person displays ignorance is not name-calling—just an observation of a lack of knowledge of what they are speaking about. In reference to the anti-gay biased pronouncements of people posting about what the Bible supposedly says about homosexuality—especially using the clobber verses—the best word to describe their lack of understanding those Bible excerpts is ignorance. A bit of study would lead someone who really wanted to understand the meaning and context of those verses to a whole different set of conclusions. I must suppose that they want to stay misinformed. By the way, I use the KJV, but when interpreting Scripture, what is likely to give the most accurate understanding of its meanings—a 500-year old English translation based on specific political agendas or the actual Greek that Paul wrote in? If we really want to know what the writers of the Bible meant, shouldn't we be trying to understand their mindsets at the time they were writing?

    pp It's all only your opinion. No facts. No proof. No study. Just your assertions...The "doctors" you quote [from the posted bibliography] are dentist... None of your facts are proven or accepted... And your personal attacks are based on falsehoods... This is all you want. To accuse and defame...

    None of what I've said is my opinion—it comes from mainstream, current Biblical scholarship, and the thousands of neurobiologists and psychologists involved in ongoing and current research. You obviously didn't do a very good job searching for the authors I cited, since none of them are dentists.

    pp Homosexuals already have all the same rights as anyone else. What they don't have is the right to special treatment because of their sexual behavior.

    omyword That's correct - if they want to live their life heterosexually then they have ALL the same rights.

    Pp, what special treatment? You want to use your interpretation of the Bible to claim Jesus was defining all forms of marriage when he never made that claim. You are using an *ipse dixit* argument (you say it yourself) that no credible Biblical scholar would consider reasonable. It does serve the purpose of letting you think gays shouldn't be married, but it's not what Jesus is saying. In point of fact, Jesus said nothing about gays.

pp Tony, you are a hateful one, it seems. Your hatefulness being why I responded. I never said "If they live heterosexually". You added that. It's totally false. Too sad...

Again, you take things out of context. Omyword was the one commenting on your saying that homosexuals had all the same rights as heterosexuals—an obviously erroneous statement. Calling me hateful when I point out the errors in your logic does not constitute a relevant argument on your behalf. But it does raise an interesting question: If you can't read a post on this thread without getting wrong who said what and why, how can you claim a superior interpretation of Scripture? Doesn't seem plausible to me.

pp Another lie. I never said that the behavior of homosexuality was not listed as a sin. It is. I said that the word homosexual didn't appear in the Bible while of course the definition of it did. See, you lie, lie, lie... You make whatever you have read change just a bit to suit yourself. Folks are on to you, dude... You have no degree. Your "doctors" are dentists that you quote. ALL of recorded history is against your personal and unsupported twistings and turnings of the Word of God. You are no scholar. You don't believe in the God of the Bible nor the Christ testified to by Paul and the other Apostles.

Let me see if I got your thoughts right here: "I am a liar who lacks evidence of my assertions being supported by credible scientists. I am uninformed on Biblical scholarship, I don't believe in God, and my relationship with God and the Scriptures isn't right (as you know right to be)." Did that cover it, pp? Not a very rational analysis of the arguments I've been making. Try again.

pp I'll stand by it...I have many homosexual friends and they tell me they don't need you defending them and that you are an embarrassment. They can take care of themselves and I haven't noticed a one who was incapable of expressing themselves. They say your brand of homosexuality is the most damaging to any message they would try to put out there since it is so self-loathing that it seeks to change the whole world rather than simply admit that your own worth is really up to you and not anyone else. Their words, not mine... *** Being in the music business I associate with homosexuals and so-called bisexuals all the time. Rather than answer yet more false accusations of yours, I will only say that if you implied that I hate homosexuals to the group of them I know, THEY WOULD LAUGH YOU TO DERISSION!!!

Let me see if I can summarize your point: Your gay friends tell you that your attitude toward them is loving and more gay-friendly than my message. They tell you that I am expressing a form of self-loathing that is damaging for them. Have I got that right? Wow! Denial ain't just a river in Egypt! The fruit is on the tree, pp, and from here it looks like yours has root rot. By the way, you referred to "my brand of homosexuality." What brand is that, pp?

dd Tony, I couldn't care less what a false prophet thinks of me. You think gays should be proud of who they are and not hide, right? Well...ok. I have decided though, I am going to be who I am and not hide it anymore. Yes, I did procreate the "natural" way and am very proud of the fruits of my efforts, namely my children. Should I be ashamed of them, because they are a product of my heterosexism?? So, since the gays want special treatment for being gay, I want special treatment for being straight...then we can all get along just fine!! OR we could just go back to not giving a dang about who has sex with whom and minding our own business, working out our OWN SALVATION. Have you ever noticed in taking up the cause of homosexuality, you have become a persecutor of

Christians?? Did God let you in on that portion of his plan before you decided to bear this cross? Just wondering.

> **Congratulations, debbie. You've just moved into the realm of heterosexism. You've labeled yourself with this post. Too bad, I thought you were better than that.**

> **dd** Thank you, thank you very much, Judge Marconi. And for my punishment, what do you recommend? PS- Do I get a trophy or a medal or something??

> **Most of your post was full of *non sequiturs*. Who said you should be ashamed of your children? Heterosexism had nothing to do with their conception, and just what special rights do gays want? How am I persecuting Christians? I'm one myself. I know many loving, caring Christians—the majority of them, I suspect—who don't want to persecute gays, but many of whom are ill informed of either what the Scriptures really say or what homosexuality is. Calling out heterosexism and homophobia is not persecution. If you can't see that, God bless you. As I keep saying, it's not about you. You have a good mind and are capable of rising above the level of name calling and the religious hysterics some people have continued to display on these posts. Instead of trying to justify your heterosexism, just let it go. You are not the self-delusional type of person who believes they and God are on the same intellectual page. When I see others do that, while confessing (boasting about) their sins, I have to conclude that it's only a tool for establishing their right to clobber others with their infantilizing version of faith. I'll continue to say it: You're better than that, debbie.**

> **koop** Why call it marriage? Why not call it what it is, a "civil union" with all the privileges of a marriage contract. NO, by insisting on calling it a "marriage", you are insisting that a homosexual preference be "honored" with the same blessings that are conferred on the union of a man and a woman. Civil liberties

are one thing, holding to the belief that marriage is a "sacrament" is another. We can agree on one, but not the other. That is the fundamental argument....... in my opinion.

Not badly stated, but all marriage in the U.S. is civilly sanctioned. Clergy perform marriages as agents of the state, and civil unions fall into the category of "separate but not equal." I fully support your church's right NOT to perform same-sex marriages, but I want my church's right to perform them made legal. To assume a heterosexual marriage is superior to a homosexual one is an example of heterosexism. Not saying that's what you intended, but—

koop According to your response, you are saying that unless the "civil union" is performed in a church, it is not legal. I think your argument does not hold water. A "civil union" with all the privileges of a marriage contract is not made MORE legal just because it is performed in a church as part of the normal sacrament of marriage. You need to be a bit more honest in what your end game really is about. It would be the Christian thing to do.

What I am saying is that civil unions are not the same as marriage (read the California Prop 8 decision summary on that point), and the fact that you want to differentiate the two goes to my observation that this is a heterosexist stance. All marriages are civil at core, and to deny marriage to gays is a denial of their civil rights. I've made no secret that full civil rights for gays is my end game, so what's your point? One other thing by way of clarification—I don't care if a marriage is performed in a church or at a courthouse—as long as the same rights and protections are accorded to the couple whether they are straight or gay. Hope that clears this up.

pp How about we stick to this: Post the proof of your statements or admit you lied...

I did post the bibliography used in my lecture and your response was "Heh, heh, heh…" Later, you claimed I was quoting a dentist, clearly indicating that you only looked up one name without bothering to determine if you had located the proper source. It's pretty clear that you either did no serious reading of the arguments being made by the Biblical scholars I cited, or, if you did read them, that you have not been able to formulate an adequate argument to the contrary concerning their findings.

dd Well, pp. You're probably heterosexist, too. I figure, what the hey, I didn't know I was before and now that I've been diagnosed, I feel fine. Of course, I have never demanded any special requirements for my heterosexuality…in fact, I figured everyone else felt the same about being a hetero too! We're here, we're straight! We can NATURALLY procreate!!

binky I see where this is all going. Tony, I am fully versed on what the Bible says about homosexuality. I don't think that it is me that you are trying to win, and if it is don't bother. I have a good grasp of the Scriptures you are using and also understand how and why you would choose to interpret them in the way you do. It's all about your motivation. Somehow I think that is how we differ. Anyone reading these posts should realize that Tony is NOT trying to lead you to the truth, but to his OWN view point. Again, don't take his word for it, look for yourself. I'm sure there are a lot of intelligent people out there that do not need his help in understanding what they are reading.

And yet you continue to try to have others drawn to the conclusions you have already reached—that homosexuality is a sin. The points of view I'm expressing are not simply my own but the conclusions of numerous Biblical scholars. If you want to rebut the arguments I've presented, please do so, but simply saying I'm wrong isn't a very convincing refutation.

pp I only have this to say: Homosexuals in this state voted right along with all others, shoulder to shoulder, on the amendment that bans homosexual unions. How you now twist that into civil rights abuse is beyond reason. Just so's you might at last get it: Y'all lost, dude... Standing as an accuser of the brethren? I've seen lots better...

binky I'm sure we all have learned something here???? As I said before, the pursuit of truth doesn't matter to Tony. He alone will tell us what we are to believe because we are unable to do this for ourselves. He will attend your festivals to make sure you understand it just the way he wants it. Thanks for the lessons, it's really appreciated. People on both sides of the argument have really benefitted from your unbiased words. You have managed to do something nobody else has ever been able to do. You should hold your head high and realize that nobody on Earth has a better understanding of God's words than you. The amazing thing is that you have figured this all out by yourself. Maybe you should write a book. With all of your responses here you probably have a good start.

koop Tony, I am afraid that you are the one who is missing the point of this argument. Even those who are willing to "live and let live" when it comes to sexual orientation are not willing to go the next step of concluding that same sex unions are deserving of being called "marriages." As I said before, if all the same RIGHTS as the marriage contract are given to those unions, why should we be required to promote the idea that neither is superior, when in fact society does believe that heterosexual arrangements are the preferred foundation of the family unit. And please, don't give me any lectures on the divorce rate, etc.

pp You see yourself as the knight in shining armor, wresting freedom from the monster instead of the poor, poor fool riding his hack into the vane again, being tossed to the ground, rent and bleeding all in the name of a love that doesn't exist... *** Quote:

"Why should gays be given a lesser status than marriage?"
Unquote: Because that status is ARBITRARILY set by the voting populous and they said they didn't want it that way...I get paid for my music...Since this is a thread about sex, I guess I can allude to what I get for my poetry...I'll just say it is much preferred to money! CRUNCH! (watching horse and rider kicked apple cart over pie wagon by windmill vane, wincing)

"Because [marriage]...is ARBITRARILY set by the voting populous and they said they didn't want it that way..."
Which is why I am doing the kind of work that is steadily undermining the heterosexist and homophobic attitudes that have dictated this bigoted attitude. Sooo—I do continue to joust at windmills knowing that each time one knocks me down, all I have to do is get up again and chip away at the foundations of its whirly, swirly, go-nowhere mechanisms. It will fall. That's inevitable. Come visit me at the county fair in our neighboring town, and see how it's done—one civil conversation at a time.

pp I'll bet that most on here don't know that your main purpose doesn't have a thing to do with church and the Bible but is a lingering battle over the homosexual marriage amendment to the constitution that you seek to have overturned...

And the arguments for that amendment were bigoted and fear based, and one day will be overturned. The tide is against you, pp, and I wonder if you can really see it coming and if that's why you're so strident against my posts. It's no secret that I view the ignorance of Scripture that is so loudly trumpeted in far too many churches as the main stumbling block to this bit of needed social justice. I've said as such many times. You've got a keen eye for the obvious, pp.

pp It wasn't enough that folks said they didn't mind what y'all did but NO, you had to force your views on everyone so we took the step to make sure you didn't by changing the constitution.

Here's a little heads up: Y'ALL LOST THAT DEBATE AND WE PASSED THE AMENDMENT. Trying to backdoor your way into that fight is actually rather hysterical, in a sad, why doesn't the dude stop trying to fight the windmill, kind of way...

    Actually, there was no debate. The Defense of Marriage Amendment (DOMA) was put on the ballot as a tactic to get the far right vote out to help get George W. Bush re-elected. There was no organized response to the proposal because the LGBT community had not yet united in its networking. Thanks to that bigoted law being passed, several equal rights organizations were formed, and the LGBT community has come together as never before. That you would crow about being part of a hate and fear based legal action only calls into question the "friendships" you claim to have with gays. Friends don't screw each other over, treat each other as second-class citizens, and threaten them with Divine repercussions if they don't change who they were created to be. If that's love, it's the kind of love a glutton has for his lunch.

    lennie Tony, you mention more times about your superiority to all, including gays and lesbians than anyone else. You self-profess that you must rescue these people from the repression, suggesting that they are incapable of doing it themselves. It seems to me by your obsession with this post thread that you are more interested in self-gratification than in true equality. After all, you were the first to comment on your own letter thereby provoking argument. Based on your rapid responses, and anticipated comments, this is an argument you must have rehearsed beforehand.

    I've never claimed superiority, lennie, just that I'm better informed than some on the Bible verses that so many people use to marginalize gays. I don't think gays can't fight their own battles or that I am their champion. I'm one small but steady voice for civil rights, and this thread gives me just one more venue to express my views. *** My first post was designed to encourage interaction on this subject, and I purposely geared it to elicit commentary, pro and con. So far, I've posted an examination of each of the clobber verses, and no one who has attempted to criticize my stance on gay rights has addressed any of them. Heckling, claiming I'm not telling the truth, and name calling rather than reasoned responses only goes to make my point that heterosexism is the foundation of what is passing for their religious "truth." I hold that this makes a mockery of Jesus' life and teachings, and the continued posts of heterosexists and homophobes on this thread exposes them for what they are. If my responses are rapid, it's because I've heard most of these "arguments" before, and they don't hold up to scrutiny.

pp You are one of the people for which I say that being unreasoning, more reason will not sway you. There are things you believe because of the proof. There are things you believe because there is no proof. Then there is what you do in SPITE of the proof. There is nothing to address with your clobber verses...The only thing that needs to be addressed is your personal motives and your missing credentials. Well, that and the lies you spread about decent upstanding folks... I almost forgot: WHACK!!!

momzy Let's get real here...gays and lesbians are discriminated against and made fun of in lots of circles, including many so alleged evangelical circles. It's a heated subject and everyone has an opinion. Almost as divisive as politics. But let's not pull the wool over our eyes and act like the gay and lesbian community is treated equally regardless of whether you agree with them. Tony, may see you at the fair.

That'd be nice, momzy. *** **Lennie, read the last few posts by pp then tell me about my feeling superior and my rehearsed responses. This is the level of discourse that passes for intellectual exchange by the heterosexists who claim to have a lock on Biblical truth. As I noted before: The fruit is on the tree, but some of it looks like it's suffering from blight.** *** **"WHACK?" I guess that means something to pp.**

momzy Tony, I do believe it is the government's responsibility to ensure all Americans have equal treatment. That is my secular point of view. Many people are passionate about their religious views. *** No matter what church you belong to....this is the mirror God had given us to see what our individual fruit looks like. It has nothing to do with whether or not I accept anyone of different religions or beliefs. It has everything to do with what is brewing in one's heart.

pp My eyes welled with tears as I thought, "Forgive [them] Lord for [they] don't know that the real Blessing isn't in the car but in the fact that I am sober enough to have a license to drive it."

lennie How can you have equality with classification, be it, self-classified or civil? Equality by definition is "rights, treatment, quantity, or value equal to all others in a specific group." So, if you are going to segregate yourself from others by self-classification, how then do you expect to be equal? That leads me to my next question; is it equality you seek or just the right to be married? If it is marriage you seek and only legal marriage, for civil liberties, why must it be a religious fight, with interpretations of the Bible used as swords? Finally, if it is true equality you want, then why do you not fight for the rights of all to be married? Would it not be okay for two straight men or two straight women to be "married" in order to have the advantages that come with marriage, such as tax breaks, health care and more.

pp Hit the nail right on the head, lennie! Well said indeed! I suggested that as a solution, that every person could choose one person to inherit and put on their paid insurance and all but "NOOOO..." that was unacceptable. Unacceptable since it didn't FORCE a certain view upon others... *** Here's the rub: homosexuals can live with whomever they please and can call themselves whatever they please and they can leave their property to whomever they please and all...Married folks can do things that unmarried folks can't do. Is that fair? Well, since I'm not married, I am "oppressed" by marriedism or whatever name t would invent! What [Tony] has never gotten is that I'm every bit the "victim" of marriage as any homosexual simply by being single!!! *** That's why it is a lie to say that homosexuals are NOT afforded every right that I am: I'm single!!! I get NONE of the benefits the married get just like every homosexual...*** All us single folks are EXACTLY equal with all the homosexuals... If a homosexual is allowed to name someone on their insurance then it is discrimination to not allow me to name a person of my choice. If it is legal for a homosexual's property to be given to their lovers, it is discrimination for the law to NOT let a straight inherit mine...So, after all the wrangling, we get to the truth of the matter and that is that it isn't at all about equality and rights but is about discrimination against straight singles!!! *** His "couplism" is all about placing the legal and social status of the couple above that of the single!!! It is allowing couples to choose whom they enfranchise legally and socially while prohibiting me from choosing a straight person from inheriting from me or being on my insurance. Like I said from the start, t isn't at all about what he says he is. His aims have nothing to do with his stated aims. All smoke and mirrors and lies about the persons of those who can see his subterfuge...

Your argument, pp, is based on a faulty premise that ignores the fact that you as a single, straight person can have all the legal rights and protections that go with marriage if you choose to undertake that commitment. Gays do not enjoy that privilege. Your argument is so laden with heterosexist bias that is makes little sense. If all this argumentation isn't about your phobia toward letting gay people get married, then please explain why you should be so concerned about the legal marital status of gay people. It couldn't possibly affect your life, so why are you so adamant in your opposition to it? The straw man you create is absurd on the face of it as I, unlike you, have never stood in the way of any person's civil rights, gay or straight; married or single.

If health care is an issue for you, work on it, but don't try to play the victim card at gays' expense.

pp I guess with all their success they'll be coming for me soon, huh? There'll be this wave of humanity storming the Capitol to overturn the amendment to the constitution? Hold your breath... *** My argument is and always has been that I do not enjoy the rights of the married and homosexuals do not enjoy the rights of the married SO THE HOMOSEXUAL AND I ARE EXACTLY EQUAL IN THAT REGARD!!! Great God in Heaven, DID YOU FINALLY GET IT THAT TIME???? *** Since the homosexual and I are in every way equal, I am oppressing NO ONE!!! *** My other point has been that IF the married are oppressing the homosexual then they are ALSO oppressing me! It simply shows your argument up for what it really is and that is seeking special privilege to discriminate against us singles... *** (windmill vane swinging toward haggard mount and rider) WHACK!!!

This is a joke, isn't it? Or is this really your actual argument? Take a look, pp, because if you're serious about this claim, you just WHACKed yourself.

pp It is based upon the same reasoning you proffer...If what I say is ridiculous then what you say is ridiculous...It's simple: You say homosexuals are discriminated against by the married because they don't have the same rights at the married. Neither do I, so I must be discriminated against as well. If I am not discriminated against, neither are they. If it is establishing special rights for me as a single person to endow me with all the rights of marriage for a straight person of my choice of my own sex, then it is endowing a homosexual with special rights as well. Sex has nothing to do with it, legally.

Your argument comes down to this: *I want to victimize gays by denying them the right to marry. I choose not to be married, therefore I am a victim, too (at least in my own mind). Therefore* *gays and I have equal rights because we are both victims.* *** I'm giving you the benefit of the doubt and assuming you can't understand your fallacy. You have the right to marry if you choose. Gays do not, and for whatever reason, you don't want them to have the choice. The correct comparison is that one of you is given a choice, the other is not. If you can't see that then the problem isn't just your attitude toward gay rights, it's in your logic.

pp That's the whole point! It isn't that the whole world of scholars spanning TWO THOUSAND YEARS disagrees with you, it's what YOU THINK is all that matters and all else is to be ridiculed...It doesn't matter that an OVERWHELMING MAJORITY WHO VOTED CHOSE TO MAKE MARRIAGE WHAT IT IS, it's what YOU THINK is all that matters and all else is to be ridiculed...I could go on...Think I'm afraid if it helps you...

If our outreach at our fair booth were the only thing being done in this state and this nation to overturn the Fear of Other People's Marriage Amendment, pp, you might be able to breathe easy. But we're only one small group out of tens of thousands of groups nationwide who are working for this cause. We've already gotten the message to the majority of 18-35-year olds, and are nearing the 50% total of the 35-55-year-old range. It's just a matter of time and effort before this sordid chapter of gross discrimination gasps its last breath.

lennie There are many advantages to marriage: taxes, health care benefits, immigration.. surely I'm not telling you anything you don't already know if you are promoting gay marriages. It goes back to my earlier post with what it is you are seeking.

Let me offer a challenge to any straight married persons out there—not as "gotcha," but as an interesting eye opener. You've all read my references to my wife—something I do as a kind of cultural shorthand. I often try not to use the word "wife" but use "partner" instead. The challenge is this: Try going for a week describing your spouse as your partner. Eliminate the words "husband" and "wife" from your vocabulary for just one week. Or try it for just a day then tell me if you think domestic partnerships are the same as marriage or if gays are being treated equally under the law. *** I'm not trying to be a wise-guy here. As I said, it's an eye-opener as to just how big a role the status of marriage plays in our culture. I guarantee that it will give you a whole new perspective on what heterosexism does to its intended victims.

omyword It was just the other day on the news a lesbian couple had their home burned down because they are lesbian. QU**** was spray painted on the garage. You don't generally see anyone painting "STRAIGHTS" on a house or garage and then trying to burn them out. I don't recall seeing anything like that. You?

Great point, omy. And if the people who use the Bible as a club don't think they are contributing to this culture of hate by the way they behave in their churches, they are deluding only themselves.

pp I've never burned down a single house...I've never fired anyone for being homosexual...Never beaten anyone for it either...

And yet you persecute gays in your own way—especially by adding your voice and vote against their civil rights. I'm still waiting for you to tell us why you think it's so great that you were part of a majority of voters who trumpeted their heterosexist attitudes by passing an anti-gay marriage amendment to this state's Constitution. Your argument that historical attitude is on your side makes about as much sense as that of slave owners who made the same type of claims to justify their position. They used the Bible, too. Paul tells slaves to be obedient to their masters and used a slave borrowed from another. Paul, of course, was a product of his culture, but to use him today to justify heterosexism is neither appropriate nor Christian in attitude.

goodfella Please be aware as Tony talks about his interpretation of the "clobber verses," they are not the only view. Also, those who hold other views than his are not always uneducated, unenlightened bigots. The challenge I have with Tony, is his presentation is often more militant and pushing his agenda than conversational.

I tried the conversational approach in an earlier God vs. Gays thread and was treated to a great deal nastiness by the you-know-who's of the newspaper's posts. I was new to this venue, and I mistakenly thought that it was possible to have polite, informed conversations. From the get-go, the straw man attacks began, and even you, gf, started in by calling me ignorant without explaining your reason for doing so. I was working and otherwise limited in the time I had to devote to the thread, but I downloaded and eventually read the 35+ small print pages on the website you recommended. Then I tried to engage you in a conversation about them, but you refused. Instead, you suggested that I might hold heretical views (shades of Middle Age thinking!) and suggested that I felt persecuted and was wrong for insisting that context is everything when interpreting the actual meaning of the Scriptures. Then you bowed out of the conversation. Gf, I've offered to sit down and have a civil face to face conversation with you on this subject, but you've refused. There are several reasons why the website you cite is far from a complete dialogue on gay marriage. As you noted, not all persons interpreting the clobber verses are uneducated or unenlightened, but they are usually as heterosexist as you can get. Gf, you may find my approach on this thread to be militant, but I'm not making the mistake I did before of not calling posters out when they persist on going down the path of persecution then insisting they're being reasonable as they continue to bash gays or to contribute to the atmosphere of heterosexism that endangers LGBT people. *** Gf, you came on that earlier thread as if you were the model of tempered reason, but you continuously jabbed at me because I disagreed with your Christology. I failed to call you out on that before, but on this thread, you don't get a free ride. Others don't like what I'm saying or how I'm saying it, yet don't offer disingenuous "civility." They are quite out front with their attacks. Others disagree with me quite respectfully and we exchange viewpoints easily (many times on private messages because they don't like the you-know-who's constant childish attacks). I personally don't mind being the one to remind those people who want to dump on gays then go all defensive when I tell them they are being heterosexist that this thread really isn't about them. I can and have been civil, but I will not accept the ignorance of heterosexists without confronting it head on.

   lennie I still think you are in it for the gratification. I can't believe that if the repressed are in numbers you have suggested, that not one person on this thread has "come out" as you say.

   blue ac Happiness in the pursuit of one's goals is gratifying, no doubt about it. Maybe the gay audience here doesn't feel inclined to out itself to the torch-and-pitchfork mob.

   That'd be my guess, blue. Why would anyone want to make themselves targets of more of the crap that some on this thread throw out here with such obvious invective? *** And even if what you think about me is true, lennie, how does that change the dynamic of how LGBT people are treated so shabbily? This thread has held more than a few examples of those attitudes and behaviors. Why not quit trying to find fault with the messenger and make a personal stand for social justice for gays?

   binky I wonder, if a person decided that they wanted to marry their pet, if that would be considered OK with the gay community? What if a person wanted to marry their son, daughter, mother, or father, would that be OK also? What if a Christian wanted to marry a non-Christian would that be OK? In the eyes of a gay person is there anything that is considered intolerable? In any of the situations above, the likelihood that the person loves their pet or relative is highly likely. I know there are companies that drop insurance on a parent's children once they have reached a certain age. Should it be OK for them to marry their children for the sake of the benefits? Why should a person be limited to one spouse? Are there not sects of the Mormon church that believe it is OK to have more than one wife? If a new church existed that said it would marry any of those listed above, would they be considered legitimate in the eyes of the gay community?

    blue ac Nice clinic on straw man fallacies.

    binky Tony, I have family that are Mormons. I'm very serious about that. At one time I too was a Mormon, but was excommunicated. I'm sure my family believes that polygamy is wrong and I do too. Do you think polygamy is wrong?

    lennie Binky, don't expect Tony to respond to any questions not in the script. Especially if it relates to the reason the marriage is sought. He is also very bigoted; he only cares about the rights of one group. Tony, you have given me no legitimate reason to join your cause.

    gf Well I got what I thought...Tony's interpretations of our past interchanges that I could try to address and get sucked into a debate with no positive outcome or ignore.

    madbuddy Tony, I personally want to thank you for the work you are doing for our rights. If I lived closer I would pay a visit to your booth.

    You're welcome, and I do it for all of us—even the heterosexists who don't get it now and may not ever. I'm not concerned whether or not you join my cause, lennie. If same-sex marriage is legalized, and two straight men or women want to get married for whatever benefits they think it will give them, then so

what? Are you implying that this should be a consideration as to whether or not we grant gays the right to marry? *** Simple question to gf—are you ready to engage in a conversation about this website, or are you just suggesting a reading list which you then will refuse to comment on any further? If that's the case, will you take time to read from my bibliography that is a bit more encompassing than the debate between two gay fundamentalist Christian men? There is a wider picture after all, and the abstinence-only guy had a lot of flaws in his reasoning—which I tried (civilly) to point out to you before. You made it clear then that you weren't up for that exchange. Anything change? *** If I seem a bit abrasive this time 'round, it's because I have spent so much time the last two days being reminded of the people that heterosexists continue to hurt. Both you and others seem to fall into that category, and, to date on this thread, I've seen nothing to suggest that the label doesn't fit. If I am wrong, please respond in ways that make sense and in ways that indicate you really want a civil exchange, gf. Otherwise, as Sonny and Cher said, the beat goes on...

    gf To answer you Tony, that was a nice try but as I explained... not playing this game with you again as it does not produce fruit. Your selective memory of our past exchanges aside, your lack of being able to correct me and the author of the side you disagree with... I post a debate between two men who are invested and explain themselves well so people can read it and make up their own minds without you or I telling them what they should believe.... Oh, how unreasonable I am.....

    And yet both gentlemen have presented flaws in their reasoning which a simple discussion could reveal. I believe the guy you back has a more seriously flawed presentation, but by refusing to engage on this issue, you prefer to let stand an argument for the unsupportable assertion that being born gay requires lifelong chastity to fulfill God's will. This, of course, reinforces the heterosexism that ultimately creates the second-class citizenship of LGBT people. Your silence implies consent to this condition, gf. J 'accuse.

blue ac The discussion is here, not on some link to another debate between other people.

gf This is what I was talking about before. I say my piece and am ready to let it go and Tony tries to suck me back in. If I don't get back in the ring for another round then I must be saying whatever he redefined me as. Seriously? Again, I've said my piece... I appreciate people checking out both sides who decided to...Outside of that, I think I'm good.....

Sorry, gf, but if, in your authority as a preacher, you lead your parishioners to the conclusion that homosexuality is a sin then they go out and vote against the civil rights of gays because of that belief system you fostered, you bear the responsibility of not teaching them better. You either are or aren't heterosexist, and trying to play neutral is not only a cop out, it's a disingenuous insult to those trying to establish social justice. When gays continue to suffer from the civil injustices encouraged by our churches, the leadership of those churches bears the responsibility to educate them. Of course, that can't happen if the leadership turns a blind eye to its own bigotry.

koop I dropped out of this thread when Tony wouldn't answer the question, "Why call it marriage, why not call it what it is, a civil union with all the rights and privileges of a marriage contract?" The key words were, "all the rights and privileges of the marriage contract." That is when I realized his arguments were circular. His argument for same sex marriage is much like a black man saying that, "equal rights are not enough, because he is still not white." I would also add that it is foolish to be drawn into an argument about how to interpret what the Bible has to say about homosexuality. People have deeply held religious beliefs on this subject that cannot be so easily described as homophobes. Yet this seems to be Tony's main argument.

Something I keep hearing about this town and its predominant attitude toward gays is how intimidating it is. That's an almost universal theme I heard at the local festival from both straight allies and the gays who spoke with us. It's also a theme I hear from sympathetic ministers who share with me that they "have to be cautious" about speaking out against the anti-gay biases in their churches. I would think some of you posters would be disturbed to keep defending this *status quo* and arguing for the right of people to be so ignorant about how Scripture is interpreted and used. I recently saw a photo from NASA showing two galaxies colliding into each other. Scientists estimate that this process started about 100 million years ago—a blink in the cosmic eye so to speak. In those two galaxies, billions of suns with uncountable planets are being destroyed while simultaneously, new suns and planets are and will be formed. On some of those worlds, there is a strong likelihood that life exists and will be destroyed. And just as possible, new life will emerge and evolve to glimpse and be a part of this majestic and incomprehensible process that is part of the whole of that which we call God. To mentally/emotionally connect for even the briefest moment with this overwhelming and glorious process is to experience awe at the reality of mankind's almost insignificant place in the cosmos. And in this context, does anyone really want to argue that the Creator actually cares who falls in love with whom—even if you want to take the uninformed notion that being gay is a choice? *** Isn't it time to get real here? Isn't it time to get past the prejudice and the nastiness that goes with it because of a half dozen verses written for a culture that no longer exists? Being gay doesn't separate anyone from God. But persecuting LGBT people sure as heck does. Feeling superior to or afraid of them does. Isn't it time to knock it off?

lennie I thought your purpose was to have people join your cause? What is the term for your superiority over me and anyone else who simply doesn't bow at your feet and unconditionally agree with you? Oh, that would be hypocritical. And yes, that should be a consideration. Your condescending tone indicates you don't agree with any reasoning for that scenario. But yet you've never answered why an "acceptable" same sex marriage is sought. Enjoy your view from the soap box. To have discussion you must also listen and I'm not sure you possess that ability.

koop Like I said Tony, your statements to defend your position are circular. When equality is agreed on to be a desirable state for everyone, but insisting on a label such as marriage for same sex unions, reveals your true motives. Sorry, you lose your veracity on this subject.

So where is the equality when marriage is limited to heterosexual couples and gays get something else? When have my motives for both gays and straights to have the same access to marriage rights been hidden? I don't know what equality means where you come from, but for me, it means everyone gets the same thing. Would you be content if gays got to call it marriage and straights were granted civil unions under the conditions you would apply to gays?

gf In my authority as a pastor, I am accountable to teach the truth and love at the best of my ability and understanding whether or not it agrees with you. I am accountable to God. There are several things you attribute to me that are not what I believe, teach or do, but it seems you are looking for targets to hammer your point on, and since I do not care to play your particular games, I'm an easy target. I can live with that. Interesting, I stated my belief a couple times and yet you accuse me of trying to be neutral? I post a place where someone who believes as I do and someone who believes as you do (or at least close) and let people read it without me pushing my points, without ripping apart the Side A gentleman, and giving respect to both as homosexual, Christian men (bigotry?) and yet you still try to paint me with your paintbrush. Oh wait.... you are good! You sucked me back in..... you are a crafty one.....

dd OK... I have just one more question...if the booth you've been posting from is soooo busy at the fair...how do you have time to sit and post literally hundreds of responses??? While I'm at it, I was thinking of this last night. If God intended people to be gay, why didn't he only make one sex that could reproduce with the same sex?? For example...Why didn't God make us all men or all women who were capable of sexual reproduction with each other or asexual reproduction?? Why did he choose to bestow the gift of reproduction on the type of people he created originally (i.e., a man and a woman) ? ALSO...most of us are claiming to be Christians (or at least believe in the Christian God). WHY,WHY,WHY *** WHY,WHY,WHY has God only revealed this to you TONY MARCONI??? ARE THE REST OF US NOT WORTHY?? Is it that we don't want to hear this message that God wants spread?? *** There are 7x more reported hate crimes against JEWS than ANY OTHER "SECT"... WOW!!! Sounds like a minority that may actually need some defending!!!

blue ac These are questions you should be asking of God, not Tony.

dd I have asked God...I know his answers to me. I wanted to know if God gave Tony a different answer. Then we can blame God for giving us all different interpretations of the same book and leave poor ol' Tony Marconi alone!!

If you're implying that God told you to persecute gays by acting in heterosexist ways that create second class citizenship for them, I think I'd rather stick to what the Bible says on this subject—which is nothing! *** I read the same Bible you do, dd. I just don't assume I know what God thinks or to claim inside info to what isn't said when He apparently didn't tell the Biblical writers to put it in there. I have claimed no special revelation—just a lot more study on these Scriptural verses than most of the posters here. By the way, if you are worried about ant-Semitism, feel free to take up the cause. My plate is full for now.

pp t has admitted his motives in the past. He only gets his knickers in a knot when someone reminds him of them. If you haven't seen his stated agenda, you haven't been paying attention...You won't get any answers from Tony...You're welcome to try...

I've actually stated my agenda quite openly, pp.

pp t believes as many others do that since they hear nothing from God, then no one hears anything from God. It's a form of vanity, really... "Heterosexism is the root of all evil" First Tony, chapter one, verse one... t doesn't believe God Spoke to anyone. He believes this because he believes God is a process and we aren't done inventing Him yet... God, by Definition, cannot deny Himself so He never contradicts Himself by telling one person one thing and another person the opposite...So, either neither of you heard from God, or one of you heard from Him and the other didn't but it can't be that you both did.

I hear from God all the time, pp. She sends me candy and flowers every day at work, and once a week we have a couple of drinks together at a piano bar. She always makes me pay, though. Did I tell you? She's got a dark, Middle Eastern complexion—and the best part: She's a lesbian! By the way, She doesn't like your attitude toward gays, and She said the guy who was writing on gf's post wasn't listening to her when she said, "Celebrate!" *** Seriously, pp—what makes you think I'm not in daily touch with God? Some Divine revelation? Ecstatic visions? ESP? Inquiring minds want to know. Perhaps the batteries in your Heavenly-issued hearing aid need replacing.

dd Tony likes calling everyone homophobic or heterosexist that doesn't agree with him.

omyword Is that what really happened or is that what people want to take away from it?

dd To me, that is what I garner from Tony. He feels he is right and anyone who disagree with him is heterosexist or homophobic, so much so, I'm not sure equality for gays is actually his aim. I'm thinking his goal is to label all of society for its perceived injustices. How does Tony know how gays feel about this topic?? He is heterosexual and married. Don't those two facts alone isolate those he is trying to fight for?? It does for everyone else. I am not opposed to gay marriage. I really don't care who does or doesn't get married. Never has. Tony told me that fact alone makes me NOT homophobic. BUT because I do think homosexuality is a sin...I somehow feel superior to gays and therefore I am heterosexist!! I say SO BE IT!! I am working on telling my friends about my condition and learning to live with its debilitating effects...

Dd, I only call people heterosexist and/or homophobic when they display those qualities. For instance, you have only presented yourself as heterosexist when you belied your claim to treat your gay friends as equals but then claimed superiority over them because you gave "natural" birth. Pp showed his homophobia when he expressed his irrational fear that someone was coming to get him next if gays were allowed to get married. See the difference? If not, study the examples again. You'll catch on. By the way, if you don't want to be known as a heterosexist, stop talking like one. I'll bet your gay "friends" will appreciate it.

lennie Tony, my question has always been: Why do they seek marriage? That you have never addressed (yet repeatedly claim you did). Nonetheless, you have proven that you are incapable of discussing the issue, merely forcing your opinions down people's throats. Sorry, but not biting here. Good luck. However, I think it is people like you that only drive a wedge between gays and straights and are just trying to keep the fire fueled.

Lennie, let me try to answer your question from a different standpoint: Why do straight people want to get married? Why do some of them seek civil marriage, others in a church? Each couple has their own answers to that question, but they are no different for gay people than they are for straights. People want the legal rights and protections, but they also want to publicly declare and affirm their social status as permanently bound spouses. The cultural and spiritual longing for complete acceptance of the union of two people with each other is not bound by race, religion, or orientation. If you are married, think of why you and your wife entered into that relationship, and if not, ask a married friend. Gays want the same thing, and now my question to you is: Do you think they shouldn't have it? And if not, why not?

momzy Tony...with all due respect, as I have stated before, the government should make sure all people have the same rights. That is my secular point of view. However, could you please look over the next few Scriptures I have quoted and give me your opinion. They would leave one to believe that homosexuality is a sin. It will take a few posts. Romans starts by telling us all of mankind is without excuse in its responsibility to God. *** Romans Ch. 1 N.I.V. version *8The wrath of God is being revealed from Heaven against all the godlessness and wickedness of men who suppress the truth by their wickedness...19since what may be known about God is plain to them, because God has made it plain to them. 20For since the creation of the world God's invisible qualities—his eternal power and divine nature—have been clearly seen, being understood from what has been made, so that men are without excuse.* *** SO NO ONE IS WITHOUT EXCUSE? RIGHT? *** *21For although they knew God, they neither glorified him as God nor gave thanks to him, but their thinking became futile and their foolish hearts were darkened. 22Although they claimed to be wise, they became fools 23and exchanged the glory of the immortal God* *for images made to look like mortal man and birds and animals and reptiles. *** 24Therefore God gave them over in the sinful desires of their hearts to sexual impurity for the degrading of their bodies with one another. 25They exchanged the truth of God for a lie, and worshiped and served created things rather than the Creator—who is forever praised. Amen. *** 26Because of this, God gave them over to shameful lusts. Even their women exchanged natural relations for unnatural ones. 27In the same way the men also abandoned natural relations with women and were inflamed with lust for one another. Men committed indecent acts with other men, and received in themselves the due penalty for their perversion. *** 28Furthermore, since they did not think it worthwhile to retain the knowledge of God, he gave them over to a depraved mind, to do what ought not to be done. 29They have become filled with every kind of wickedness, evil, greed and depravity. They are full of envy, murder, strife, deceit and malice. They are gossips, 30slanderers, God-haters, insolent, arrogant and boastful; they invent ways of doing evil; they disobey their parents; 31they are senseless, faithless, heartless, ruthless. 32Although they know God's righteous decree that those who do such things deserve death, they not only continue to do these very things but also approve of those who practice them. *** Our world today? your thoughts.....*

    Momzy, Paul's letter is written prior to a visit to Rome where he hopes the house churches that have been established there will fund his continuing missionary work. But these worship communities are comprised of Jews and Gentiles that are fractious and ready to split themselves apart over a very real disagreement: Are Gentiles required to follow Mosaic law—get circumcised and follow the prescribed dietary rules that the Jews do? *** Paul wants to unite, not further divide, the two groups, so he begins with a denunciation of idolatry for which God gives over the minds of the perpetrators to uncleanliness. And while in such a state of mind, they dishonor themselves by behaving "contrary to nature." This is seen by many Christians today as synonymous with homosexuality. *** But that interpretation is

questionable when we look at Paul's wording in the Greek. He uses the phrase *"para physin,"* traditionally translated into English as "against nature." But, *para physin* actually implies something "uncharacteristic." Think of the sentence, "Contrary to her nature, Jean got up and danced all night." Jean didn't violate the laws of the cosmos by her actions. She simply did something out of character for her: *Para physin.* *** The parallel of the women in verse 26 with the clearly defined lustful behaviors of the men in verse 27 is, I think, fairly clear. *** And, that said, it is indisputable that Paul's description of the *"para physin"* behaviors of men definitely does include same-sex acts. But — and this is key — in Paul's worldview, homosexuality as we know it today doesn't exist. There are only heterosexual females and males. Therefore, he is decrying lustful self-gratification by heterosexual men with other heterosexual men—not an uncommon practice in the Greco-Roman world of that era. But these behaviors are not acts of love and commitment between male homosexuals, about which Paul says nothing. *** For Paul, these *para physin* homogenital acts committed by heterosexual men are *"atima,"* which means unseemly or degrading—King James says "vile." And, they make the participants appear *"aschemosyne,"* that is, shameless or dishonorable. But they are not morally condemned. When Paul does get around to blasting the real wrongdoings and wicked behaviors of the idolaters, enumerated in Romans 1:28-31, he uses the words *"asebia"* and *"adikia,"* which relate specifically to moral, not social, offenses. *** Actually, when Paul's letter is read as a whole, its entire structure is based on the premise that he does not consider *para physin* sex to be morally condemned. Remember, Paul wants to enter into the dispute that is raging between the Jews and Gentiles, but he has to approach the issue carefully, trying not to alienate either side. *** So, first, he gains the sympathy of Jewish Christians by seeming to go along with their prejudices regarding Roman sexual practices. The Jews would have figured he had the Gentiles pegged on that one, and the Gentiles would probably have chuckled at the provincial attitude of the Jews regarding sex.

Romans were, after all, men of the world. *** But, then, Paul decries the real wickedness caused by idolatry, and he immediately reminds the Jews that even though they have the advantage of the Law concerning circumcision and dietary cleanliness, they are still guilty of their own transgressions against God. Pressing this point further, Paul argues that in Christ, purity issues are superseded. They are no longer of paramount importance. *** What Paul says, in Chapter 14, verses 13-14 is this: "Let us not therefore judge one another anymore; but judge this rather, that no man put a stumbling block or occasion to fall in his brother's way. I know, and am persuaded by the Lord Jesus, that there is nothing unclean of itself; but to him that thinks anything to be unclean, to him it is unclean." In other words, uncleanliness under Levitican law is in the eye of the beholder. *** In essence, Paul used the issue of sexual practices as a rhetorical device precisely because they didn't matter all that much in the world of his time. Isn't it ironic that the topic he picked to help him introduce his plea for unity is the one that threatens to tear mainstream churches apart today? *** I cannot stress strongly enough how important it is to realize that Paul was writing from the perspective of his time and culture. In his world, slavery was acceptable—and his words were used frequently in an ante bellum America to support the ownership of human beings. Paul lived in a time when women were, at best, second-rate persons and, at worst, mere possessions. Paul would have considered disease to be demonic in origin, long hair on men to be *para physin* and "*atima*" (shameful or degrading). He thought male genitalia to be "*aschemosyne*" (dishonorable). The concept of homosexual orientation as we understand it today was simply unknown to him. What Paul clearly commented on was what he saw according to the limitations of his 1st Century C.E. culture: Heterosexual people giving into their lusts and desires to be self-indulgent due to their continued practice of idolatry. To continue to use these verses as an excuse to marginalize gays and lesbians today serves only to remove our churches from Paul's original intent to unite them as "one body in Christ." ***

momzy Tony, lot of meat added to the bone here from Romans. I will initially agree in part that one must consider the time and context of Scripture to relate it for today's time. However, when doing that, one must be careful to not change what the intent of the Scripture says. You do make some valid points. Please check in occasionally as I will reply and hope to get some more input.

pp The fact that you are at odds with all that God Has given Mankind lets me know that you are not in contact with God. No brainer...Yes, or no: Do you HEAR God's Voice? By what authority do you presume to call all of recorded history wrong? What authority has God Bestowed upon you to tell us all we are wrong and what do you proffer to make us think it is Truth? In short, why should ANYONE listen to you??? What are YOUR revelations and what is the evidence of them??? Like I said, no scholarship, no revelations, nothing but HOT AIR!!!

There are none so blind as they who will not read. You keep asking for evidence, and I have given you a bibliography, posted detailed explanations of the clobber verses, and offered to sit face to face with you to have a detailed discussion. Your responses have been little more than inanities and tirades. I get that you feel you've been saved by God. I have no problem with that, but I do object to your insistence that everyone must come to God in accordance with your experience. That intolerance of others is what makes a mockery of Jesus' teachings.

blue ac One man's voice of God is another's schizoaffective episode.

pp Funny how that is the so called "answer" to anyone who claims that their Father Speaks to them. Funnier still are those who then "claim" to believe in the Bible which is the only testimony of exactly that thing!!! The real Test of course is when you are told that which all the Apostles of the Bible tell us: ASK HIM YOURSELF AND THEN YOU WILL KNOW AS MUCH AS ANY HUMAN CAN THAT YOU ARE HEARING FROM GOD. I KNOW what God Has and Does Tell me. I am so confident in this that if what you tell me He Told you doesn't line up with what I know He Told me, I am confident you either didn't ask or that you are not hearing God. As for the purposes of this discussion, t does not believe what is clearly written. Nor does he claim any personal revelation from God. He certainly doesn't present any scholarship of any credibility. I will remind you that if you think "Christian" means to sit back and let those who would twist and obscure the Word of God go unchallenged, I say you don't know what being Christian is.

omyword pp, I can go one for one you with Scripture but what would that solve? You obviously have missed a lot and are not free from error yourself. So yes go ahead and say only you could know the answers and I don't talk to God or hear him-how insightful of you. Tony seeks to normalize homosexual behavior in traditional evangelical circles as part of his efforts. I understand equal rights so take that off then table. What evidence is there though, that indicates homosexuality inside a church is an acceptable form of behavior from a Biblical point of view? *** I believe Tony does try to use Biblical authority as supporting his cause. I will add....that nowhere does the Scripture indicate that discrimination should occur because of gay lifestyles.

pp (replying to omyword): You say you don't speak for God and here you're speaking for God...Telling someone the blunt, unadulterated truth isn't a sin, dude...Deal with it...

omyword Not being on God's level and reiterating something from Scripture is not speaking for God. He doesn't need me to speak for Him.

pp The thing that gets my dander up the most is that you didn't get a word I said. My post was about Jesus, not myself. The fact that you then make it all about you tells me all I need to know.

omyword You make things into what you want them to be to suit how you want to see them.

pp And I like to get a thing straight every now and then. People often say that I don't "act Christian." They then denounce me for having a brain or having strong opinions or for (GASP) telling someone that they are wrong. What chaps their lips the most, I think, is that I then PROVE them wrong. So, when y'all jump up and JUDGE me for my straightforwardness, I am often brought to the passage that says that you do err, not knowing the Scriptures.

Pp, I'm pretty sure I would never have cause to denounce you for having a brain, and I certainly would never judge you for proving anybody wrong.

pp Now, one cannot say who does know God but one can most certainly say who does not! The Bible is clear that this is done by first ASKING GOD YOURSELF AND THEN GOING WITH WHAT HE TELLS YOU. I have asked many on here to ask God Himself HIS Opinion of my works and that I will accept.

Well, how convenient: If God Himself is talking to you, who are we to question your works?

pp Get off'n the cross, t, we need the wood!

Might I suggest that huge block above your shoulders? *** By the way, I just got a phone call from God. She says your religious outreach is far too toxic for Her tastes. Does this mean you'll quit preaching that your spiritual insights are superior to everyone else's? God gave me 5 to 2 odds you won't, but I didn't take Her up on it because She's prescient, you know. *** And now the

time has come for me to wrap up the Tony Marconi portion of this thread. After I'm done, you can all go back to what you were doing before I convened this adult education class. Thanks for attending. *** If my classroom manner has been—as some of you have claimed–militant, it's only because after the God vs. Gays thread, I've adapted myself to fit the mindset of the majority of those who have chosen to attend this lecture. Think of me as a mirror reflecting back much of whatever you've been posting on this and the aforementioned God/Gays thread. I'm pretty sure I said then that I had begun this thread to elicit commentary and that my responses were quick simply because after you've been in the struggle for LGBT rights for even just a little while, there really are no new questions—just those who get it, those trying to learn about it, and those who simply aren't ready to learn more, so they don't. *** The first time I tried interacting in this venue in God/Gays, I didn't understand the basic premise of the handful of trolls who lurk on these threads is that everything is about them. They aren't interested in a serious exchange of ideas either because (it seems) they are incapable of going into any depth on this topic or because there is some need in their lives to be empowered by claiming victory in this domain. *** A lot of speculation (mostly derogatory) has been posted suggesting that I have some special agenda that I am keeping secret. I thought I'd been up front about why I started this thread, but for anyone who missed it, here's the expanded version: For the last 9 or 10 years, I have focused my spare-time energies almost exclusively (with only minor distractions) on LGBT social justice issues. These posts have provided a tool for advancing this cause and affording me a link to and with other organizations doing similar work. The venues for my/our outreach are ever-expanding, and I am always seeking to get our message out in different ways. This town's festival and this thread were two new ones this year. *** This thread was my experiment to see what I could do with using it as a venue in and of itself. *** I have used this thread to reiterate an analysis of the Biblical clobber verses and to point out the problems they cause in our secular culture (created by the heterosexism that too often permeates our worship communities). *** Some of you have noted/complained about the number of posts I've been making. The complainers have missed the obvious, but that doesn't surprise me. As I said before, these threads are about them (at least in their own minds), and numbers, not quality of the potential conversations, seem to matter most in their thinking. *** I've assessed the quality of this thread over the past week or so, treating it as a learning tool and judiciously doing my homework (I spent 3 hours responding to posts on Monday night alone after 12 hours at the county fair). I've observed the patterns here in a more detailed way than I did on the God/Gays thread, and the results have been a mixed bag. The private messages I've received tell me that some of you really get it, and not everyone who contacts me bothers to respond much or at all on this public thread. So, I know that my message is being read (and appreciated) by more than just the half-dozen or so who seem to be the main responders on this site. *** Likewise, there are a few posters on this thread who see the heterosexism that is so rampant in the responses of—well, we all know who. They refuse to buy into the self-serving bullying of some posters who call themselves "Christian" but don't seem to model Jesus' teachings very well. Perhaps the greatest value as a teaching tool this thread has had is to provide heterosexists and their enablers a place where they can demonstrate in a public forum what bigotry can do to the human mind. By serving as examples of how narrow-mindedness consumes their reason, they've functioned as an interesting, if pathetic, form of classroom aid. That, too, was a part of my lesson plan: to draw certain posters out of their heterosexist closets and to allow them to rant so I could comment on their attitudes and behaviors. WHACK! *** I have noted that a few people feel like it's okay not to confront heterosexism based on their sense that the -ism that I'm fighting isn't the one they'd choose to take on themselves. Personally, I think that is a legitimate viewpoint with the caveat that all of us need to at least be trying to learn what any -ism looks like and what any -ist or -phoebe sounds like so we know it when we see or hear it. But this raises two questions that I'm going to pose to clergy members in general and gf in particular. The first is this: When you know an evil exists (in this case, heterosexism) but choose to remain silent or neutral when you are in a position to speak truth to power, doesn't that create mutual culpability in the perpetuation of that evil? *** The second question is this: Suppose one tolerates an evil that is being incubated in one's worship community because of all of the other good that would be disrupted if the church had to come to terms with its own bigotry. Then what is the acceptable ratio of evil tolerated to good applied? If you do come up with that magic formula, would you please share it with me? *** And so this thread comes to a close—at least for me. I've done all the studying of it and/or teaching on it that I care to do. As a venue, I think its limitations far outweigh its advantages. It's been interesting but too limiting to be of value to my work. If any of you want to come to a place where you can enter into civil, face-to-face conversation, you are invited to stop by our booth at the county fair this week. *** That said, class is dismissed, but feel free to hang around and talk among yourselves. *** P.S.: Remember to always act out for equality!

    gf Some lessons I wished we covered in class...Do you try to answer questions the teacher poses at you that attribute beliefs at you that you do not hold or express? Do you feel guilty when being accused of not having level headed exchange of ideas by a person who claims they are the teacher, this is their class, and you are continuing evil because you disagree with them? Can you claim all you need is love and continue to speak down at people? *** While I do believe from years of study and discussions that same gender sex is a sin (don't want to come off neutral), I believe it is no more and no less than any sin and does not affect my love for any in my life that are practicing homosexuals. I know many will not understand that and I get it, but I don't think any of us should stereotype anyone on any side of the "conversation."

pp Like I said, you don't hear from God and have the AUDACITY to call Him a her after He Used the Male pronoun Himself...If you think this drivel will dissuade me, I think the odds are more than a trillion to one that it does not... *** One here hounded me day and night for MONTHS, dude...t lays awake nights thinking up comebacks...I knew you wouldn't pray, your pride will not let you. I'm outta here. If I don't let t "win," he quits playing...Though he isn't much use for anything else, he is a good excuse to get the word out about homosexuality! And t, you made a mistake by using the "heh, heh, heh," criticism from the Gays vs. God thread: BUSTED!!! HAVE FUN WITH YOUR SPLIT PERSONALITY! BUB-BYE...Oh, one last thing, it isn't so impressive to brag about a thousand posts when 870 of them are yours, t...

dd Good post. We all try to discuss with Marconi, but you are right about the liberal agenda. We are not allowed to use labels or say things like homosexuality is a sin...but we ARE allowed to be labeled as bigots, homophobes, extremists, and my personal fave, heterosexist. Sort of a do as I say, not as I do attitude, I guess. But since us heterosexist homophobes are in the majority, we don't deserve the same rights/protections as our homosexual counterparts I guess (to not be name called, etc.). After all the gay community is defenseless against our hate. That's why Marconi has become their super hero... I can't get over that "you're a great human being and deserve defending unless you disagree with me" attitude. Then you're an evil, hate filled, heterosexist homophobe, that has no right to even utter the name Jesus...I would suggest to Tony, in the future, if you wish to draw more to your cause, lay off the names and the labels you ascribe to everyone else and just preach your message. Sort of like, you get more flies with honey than you do vinegar!

blue ac You don't really need honey to attract flies.

And why would I want to attract flies in the first place when I can surround myself by the likes of pp, lennie, puddy, koop, etc.

just by defending gay rights. Thought I was done, but the Fair is still busy, and in between visits from the general public, I've got a bit more time on my hands. OMG! I think I just saw a gay fly!!! Run—

    momzy I thought this blog had already died and been buried. But...what the hay....I'm game for another round!

    Okay, my schedule will only allow me some on and off log-in time for the next day and a half, so I'll jump in here one last time for the sake of those who have privately e-mailed or told me in person that they are following this thread and appreciate the views I've posted. My intent was, and is, to add my voice to the rising tide of those demanding social justice for gays, and that day is coming. In a max of 10-20 years, anti-LGBT views will have become the domain of an intolerant minority and will be regarded by most people as holdovers from a heterosexist past. They will be compared to racists and rightfully so. *** Let's review the issues one more time. The clobber verses I've discussed only work if they are taken out of context or if homosexual orientation is loosely defined as rape, lust prostitution, and two Jewish men engaging in a specific non-reproductive sex act. Because of that misunderstanding of Scripture, our churches enable their congregations to develop a heterosexist viewpoint that they carry into the voting booth where they institutionalize a second-class citizenship status for gays. *** So this time, why not address the issues: In what way have I misrepresented either the clobber verses or homosexual orientation, and, aside from the argument that everyone has historically thought so (same holds true for the flat earth theory), explain why your interpretation of these verses is superior. And how do you argue that our churches don't contribute to heterosexism?

gf For those who care to hear both sides: http://www.gaychristian.net/greatdebate.php

momzy Considering the views that Tony presented. It will take some time...but the study will be well worth the effort. That's the way I am going...the video cannot replace that. *** Now before everyone gets in an uproar, I'm not against fundamental Baptists. However, I know what goes on behind the scenes in some of our religious circles. Now, I think we are missing one of the points Tony makes. What do people use to justify themselves when they make fun of minorities and homosexuals. They use religion and the Bible. Tony aptly uses the term clobber verses, because that's what occurs within the self-righteous religious community. They use the Bible to clobber other people. And you don't have to look far to find them...maybe even in the mirror. Now, I know that's it's been mentioned that Christ upset others when he walked the earth. I guess you could say he 'clobbered' others. But who were they....Scribes and Pharisees and the religious leaders of that day. Who had the biggest problem with Christ? THE SELF RIGHTEOUS DID!

The only problem with gf's recommended site is that it gives a flawed view of the clobber verses by the gentleman that gf backs—both in its Greek translation of I Corinthians 6:9-10 and his rather bizarre philosophy of "complements" which is definitely not Scriptural and assumes that the writer has figured out what God actually thinks based on his need to remain celibate. Gf, once again you are enabling heterosexism by refusing to engage on this issue while at the same time promoting this one website as somehow conclusive in its discussion. Again, j 'accuse.

gf I am open to letting people study & decide without me going on about all the reasons I think the gentleman I disagree with is wrong. I think the Bible can stand up to the study. Not sure why Tony can't do the same?

The reason is simple, gf. By the very fact you've weighed in on this topic, lending weight to a certain perspective—one in which a flawed rationale is offered and, by implication, endorsed, by you as—not just the beginning of a conversation, but an end (as far as you seem to be concerned)—you've taken a stance then have refused to discuss it. This is disingenuous, whether you realize it or not. You make your point (homosexuality is a sin) by directing readers to a far from adequate conversation about the clobber verses, then refuse to engage on those very verses, claiming the discussion on that website is sufficient. As I have repeatedly stated, it is not. If you don't want to engage on the topic, quit entering the conversation obliquely or I'll keep on calling you on it. You simply can't have it both ways. You are not neutral on this subject, but you seem to imply you are. *** One other point that I've expounded on before but I think needs to be reiterated. You have the luxury of allowing this debate to languish on some remote academic level because your life isn't being made difficult because of your sexual orientation. My gay friends don't get to sit back unaffected while clergy like you refuse to take responsibility for what their parishioners do with the intolerance they are taught and/or are enabled to practice because their ministers refuse to learn what the Bible is actually talking about when it comes to sexual orientation. If you don't want to engage, fine— then don't. But you don't get to play the disembodied peacemaker while you continue to foster an atmosphere that makes other people's lives hell.

pp Here's the only issue: You are trying to cause others to throw out two thousand years of scholarship and basic common sense because you say so. You don't have a degree in Greek. You don't have a degree in comparative religion. You don't have any scholars to back you up. When confronted with this fact you toss out the name of "Dr. So And So" but when I looked up his credentials, the dude was a DENTIST. You claim no revelation from God...As for context, here it is: If you don't like it, you INVENT one that suits you. You SAY you have thousands of followers and yet when you gave your "lecture" here in our town, no one showed up. You claim hundreds at your booth but when I stopped by and spent a coupla hours watching (I was there already), all I saw was you handing a paper out that was looked at and dropped. *** Your "prophecy" is ten or twenty years into the future and yet it has been at least ten years since you made it first and in that time, Ohio passed a law against homosexual marriage rather than racing to correct what you deem a social injustice. Most of us didn't really want to do that but y'all FORCED our hand. Lastly, out of your supposed THOUSANDS of supporters you have not one who will even recommend you once. And the fact that you don't believe it does nothing to change the almost universal consensus of my homosexual friends who say you are an embarrassment and that they are quite able to speak for themselves.

Well, this is going to take awhile, so—

1) Thousands of years of scholarship: Incorrect. Modern Biblical scholarship is only about 200 years old. It has progressively revealed truths about the Bible that don't jive with your infantilizing version of faith. Research into sexual orientation is only about 150 years old and our more in-depth understanding about sexual orientation about fifty. The fact that my pamphlet lists six Biblical scholars and Britain's foremost neurobiologist and you confused at least one of them with a dentist says loads about your "scholarship."

2) I never said I have a degree in Greek, but a number of the scholars I cite do. I do not claim revelation from God. I've stated dozens of times that you give no evidence other than your insistence that you do speak for the Deity that you have had such a revelation. People who insist that they know what God thinks (as you insist that you do) are not, in my opinion, either believable or rational. So far, your animosity has had you do nothing more than rave at me while displaying your lack of fact of either Biblical context or social injustice.

3) I've never claimed thousands of followers—just that our booths have seen that many visitors. And by the way, people did attend my lecture in town, and your description of our booth's activities is patently false. Again, your credibility is questionable.

4) No one forced the voters to adopt the bigoted defense of marriage amendment. There were already laws on the book defining marriage as a union between a man and a woman. The amendment was a hate-filled, reactionary measure designed for political purposes, and you endorsed it and continue to trumpet your heterosexism. Yeah, you've got gay friends. *** When have you addressed the clobber verses and their effect on the heterosexism in our churches? Those were the issues on this thread from my first post. Having failed to actually engage on those topics, and being unable to do any kind of valid research and/or checking of the sources I cited, you created straw man arguments and when those failed to score points for you, you've resorted to outright lies. I think there's a Commandment about bearing false witness, but maybe in one of God's revelations to you, He exempted you from it.

5) You insist you spent hours skulking around our booth, but if this were true, we would have seen you as we usually have a pretty clear view of people in the vicinity. Another lie, pp? By the way, you seem a bit obsessed with my outreach work. If you had really been in the vicinity of our booth, you could easily have come up and engage in a conversation. Instead, you seem to think it does you credit to claim you stalked us. Weird, don't you think?

The question I am forced to consider is this: Why is it so important to you that homosexuality be a sin? If right and wrong are in God's court, why are you so intent on making homosexuality a wrong? If Scripture isn't supposed to be interpreted by man, shouldn't basic definitions of what constitutes homosexuality be compared to what the Bible is actually speaking of? And if the Bible is the actual Word of God, shouldn't we be using every tool of understanding to get that Word right? Absent scholarship, the only thing you propose is that we ask God to tell us what is right or wrong. *** Well, pp, you're not the only one who has asked Him, and when others get different answers, you fuss and fume. The problem with your argument is that you insist we all ask God to reveal the Truth about homosexuals, but you do nothing to enhance your understanding of the actual written Word that would enlighten you on the subject. Your argument comes down to this: I'm right, I hold a majoritarian view, therefore God has spoken the Truth only to me and those who think like me. Doesn't work, pp.

    pp If there is anyone out there homosexual or otherwise who wishes to serve God, look to Heaven and ask Him with a humbled heart and if He Chooses to Speak, listen to Him and Him Alone, for in the End we will ALL stand before Him and His Judgment! *** Not by pontifications and twisted "context" but by standing and boldly declaring before all what God Has Done in your life!

    Many gays already do have a close relationship with God and have accepted Jesus Christ as their personal Savior. They are born again and don't buy into your interpretation of their "sins." But your attitude represents a stumbling block for them and many others who have been driven from their worship communities by people like you. Since I have not twisted either the context or meaning of the clobber verses, all of your evangelical pronouncements (glorifying your supposed superior relationship with God) ring hollow. *** You have the opportunity to replace the batteries in your Heavenly-issued hearing aide, but you'd rather cling to ignorance about the actual meanings of the clobber verses and the unchristian things people do because they refuse to learn more about them and what homosexuality really is. No human mind can comprehend the majesty of God in Its Totality. That you assume you do tells me right away that you are speaking for yourself, not Him. You are like one of the blind men examining the elephant and assuming your portion of the animal is its whole. Big mistake, pp. And, by the way, your fervor only serves to make me wonder just what part of Dumbo you've got hold of. *** Really, pp, you are moving rapidly from the realm of poor reasoning to the world of bizarre delusion. What next? Ecstatic visions? Angelic annunciations? You're not planning any trips to Damascus in the near future, are you?

gf Questions: Can a person think that same gender sex is a sin according to the Bible and not treat people in the GLBT community with hatred and contempt? Can you believe the Bible states this and still be the Good Samaritan and love and care for someone who is gay? Can someone have family members who are gay and still believe the Bible says that same gender sex is a sin? And can people in the GLBT community have friends and family members who hold this belief and love them? Is it all or nothing.... either a person is an advocate or a hater?

I think you pose a valid question, gf, and my answer is: no, it's not all or nothing. Momzy sets a good example of how this is true. He acknowledges the evil caused by heterosexism, and he treats the homosexual the way the Good Samaritan treated the Jew— seeing only the man in need and caring for him. But that's not what is going on in far too many of our churches. On any given Sunday, how many Christians are "treated" to sermons on the sin of being gay. And the sad truth of the matter is that a little learning about what sexual orientation is and why it is not addressed in the Bible, could alleviate so much suffering. *** I would think that Christians would rejoice that they no longer had to be responsible for hurting gays—and many do. But too many persist in refusing to learn about same sex orientation. If they don't understand that, then it is easy for them to continue to marginalize gays. *** A follow up question, gf: Is it all or nothing with racism? Creedalism? Sexism? Again, the issue comes down to education on two things: What is homosexual orientation and what does the Bible say about it. *** The answer to both requires an understanding of the function of sex in the emotional and spiritual development of human beings. Our capacity to love, cherish, and be fulfilled through the intimacy of bonds that are often the outcome of sexual unions—physical and/or emotional/spiritual—is part of what makes us fully human. For 95% of the human population, genetic/hormonal combinations trigger heterosexual attractions. In 5% they cause same-sex attractions. Neither is a matter of right or wrong; it is how we were created to be. The Bible says nothing about committed, homosexual relations. It condemns only the misuse of this capacity with rape, lust, prostitution, and a specific non-procreative act for Jews. *** So, again—what is this need for so many Christians to have homosexuality be defined as a sin? If it's not their sin, they need to get out of the judgment business as Jesus told us to do. If it is a sin, then the sin is between the sinner and God without the benefit of third party commentary. And never should anyone's civil rights be determined by another person's perception of their state of grace with God. This attitude is reprehensible and abhorrent to anyone with a desire to see social justice for all. "We, the people," means all of us. Remove the beam from thine own eye applies to all of us. When our churches stop preaching ignorance, maybe people will get their personal abhorrence and obsession with gay sex out of the ballot box. Our churches bear the responsibility to lead people to the light—not the darkness of ignorance and misinformation. *** Gf, as a person who understands the evils and who leads a flock, the responsibility to enlighten falls more heavily on you.

    gf Thanks for the answer Tony though I think your actions sometimes portray a different thought. Outside of that, the framing of the arguments you give tend to be more about how you win a fight instead of what is the real question. Maybe we all do that. I don't know. My quest is to find the truth in the Bible no matter what the topic, including sins, and then finding the life application through love without negating truth. Not sure why you feel that Christians decide homosexual sex is sinful so they twist and turn to make the Bible back their hate. Anyways, I'm jumping back off. I'm on vacation and my laptop battery is dying. Oh, and yes, I do preach from the Word on both Truth and Love. It is a heavy responsibility but when God leads..... quite a blessing....

Gf, I, too, seek the truth in the Bible, so we have that in common. It remains, however, my personal belief that seeking the truth will eventually result in a win-win situation where, as Christians, we gain a better understanding of that truth and that will lead us to realize that we should fully include gays and gay rights in both our churches and our civil lives. *** And with this, dear thread junkies, I must take my leave. Amazing—3 letters and a total of over 1500 posts. Though not always on topic, I've been personally pleased to have had this opportunity to express my views. Hope you have, too. (Even you, pp.)

A Brief Dialogue On Faith

The God vs. Gays threads led to a dialogue on the nature of faith in general and Christianity in particular. This thread, conducted mostly between two former posters, Goodfella and Momzy, and myself took on a very respectful tone, and provided much food for thought. The following conversations have been edited to reflect only those exchanges, ruling out the few, half-hearted attempts by Debbie Diamond and Pistol Pete to revert back to the former topic. The three of us refused the bait, and continued our exchanges for several weeks.

Momzy: Tony....just wondering how, from a Biblical-Scriptural perspective, you can develop a theology that does not have a "judged afterlife"? If I can provide direct and indirect statements from Scripture, that indicate such places exist, I am curious as to your views. *** Your historical perspectives/narratives on ancient cultures and civilizations are spot on. But that would not necessarily give me insight into spiritual matters. It only tells me how a specific group of peoples lived/believed from a historical perspective. I believe the difference lies in perspective. My theology has been developed using a systematic approach. (Everyone has a theology—they just don't know it). As my starting point, I use the Presuppositional approach which says there is one God and the Bible is His Word. The primary purpose of Creation and Scripture is to reveal Him.

Momzy, like academic knowledge, our faith is able to grow by increasing our understanding. When I was a kid, the concept of Jesus as God could have been explained by substituting the words "Jesus Christ" into the song "Santa Claus is Coming to Town." And, like author and Biblical commentator Mel White says, "There's nothing wrong with having a 5th grade understanding of God—as long as you're in the 5th grade." For me, faith is a

lifelong exploration, and without unanswered questions, it wouldn't be—well, faith.

Momzy: Levels of authority must be assigned when making theological statements. I use the six-level model. The levels are Direct statements, then Direct Implications, next Probable implications, Inductive Conclusions, Conclusions Inferred from general revelation and lastly...Outright Speculations! *** I avoid a flat theology which does not distinguish between levels of authority. For example, you'll find no direct statements of authority regarding the Trinity. But I can show you direct implications using Scripture that give credence to this doctrine! *** Let me back up to the perspective issue. If I were to send you into a 40-acre woods and tell you that somewhere in there was a buried chest full of gold, and if you found it, you could keep it. *** First, wouldn't you want to know how credible I was in making this statement? (faith) If Bill Gates took you to the woods versus me, wouldn't you get a better warm and fuzzy with Bill? Now, Bill could be lying, but somewhere faith comes in, right? *** Sitting squarely on the faith issue for now, before I bust off to the woods: I could consult 50 people about Bill's honesty. I could look up financial stats to determine if Bill Gates did indeed have the money! I say I...I mean you...sorry about the switch. *** So now I am down to a couple of issues. First...do I put trust in what the guy said? If so, off I head to the woods. Now, given it's hunting season let's say you run into a couple of deer hunters. *** Let me switch again...suddenly I realize my search is a whole lot different than the hunters because of my perspective. In fact, it completely changes how I view the woods and how I conduct my search with respect to the hunters. They have guns and hide in/behind the trees. I got my large metal detector and shovel. We are all in the same place but searching for different things. *** I see the woods as a place to find riches beyond belief. The hunters see the woods as a food source. (By the way, the hunters placed faith that deer would show up!) *** All that is to say that when I come to the Bible, I realize it is the only source in which God has revealed Himself as well as a historical account as to how he has dealt with civilization and specifically Israel. I'll end right now at the starting block of truth. FAITH. Everyone has it. It might be faith that there is no God. It might be faith in Hinduism or any -ism. As you said 'T', you have faith that there is no afterlife. We all have faith in something! *** The question is, and it's an important one, do you trust your faith to sustain you the instant you take your last breath. We all will know! If there is no God or afterlife, all is well so to speak. If someone has faith they will go to Heaven because they made a 1-line Bible track confession in Christ but lived a life of hell raising...ok. If someone has faith ALLAH will reward them for blowing themselves up and killing infidels...ok.

    Momzy, you post an excellent example, and I think the answer to your question comes down to the issue of what authoritative weight one is willing to give Scripture and/or to which parts. For me, saying that the Bible is the word of God doesn't mean that it was "faxed" down to the authors of its books. I suspect that you already know much of how the Bible came to be in its myriad current incarnations. As a person raised as a Christian, the Bible holds a great deal of significance for me as a way of understanding how our Western culture developed its predominant understanding of humanity's relationship with God. Had I been born a Muslim, I would have come to that understanding through the Koran—which I would have regarded as the ACTUAL word of God, spoken directly by an angelic messenger to Mohammed. When I read the Bible, I try to understand it as fully in its contexts as possible, with the knowledge that it's a progressive work composed by men of different times and circumstances, responding to specific sociological conditions. Are they Divinely inspired to write down their interpretations of their specific situations? Of course! Does that mean that they were omniscient and could foresee all things that would happen in the future? Not in my opinion. It is not hard to make the Old Testament "reveal" the centrality of Jesus when the people writing about Jesus are going back looking for OT passages that will point to just that. Before even one word about Christ had been written, there was a generation of Jews who discussed this person and his message in the synagogues and who was finding evidence that he was, indeed, the Son of Man. Mainstream Jews rejected this—I mean, how was Jesus supposed to be the Messiah if he was an executed criminal? The answer, of course, was to reinterpret the Messiah's purpose, and that reinterpretation ultimately created a new religion—thanks to Paul and a few persons of note. *** But the process that brought about orthodox Christianity and its authorized canon was a long and contentious fight, and it is still ongoing today. You said, "*As my starting point, I use the Presuppositional approach...there is one God and the Bible is his Word.*" I think most Christians would agree with you. Obviously, I differ in as much as I am an existentialist who believes we all define our own lives. It really isn't such a huge jump to go from there to an un-judged theology—an understanding of God as Process and Jesus as the connection through which I personally find the best fit. As you pointed out, you can find a Scriptural basis for any point you want to make. But, for me, I want to know two things: 1) How close to the original author's meaning can we come, and 2) Is the mindset of the original author actually relevant to our lives and understanding of God today? (Witness Leviticus 12.) *** You raise the critical issue that separates peoples of faith into those who believe in a judged afterlife and those who do not. I want to be specific—I used the word "judged" in the way I think mainstream Christianity uses it. For me, as to whether or not something comes after, I don't profess to know—but I do have enough faith in the God Process to believe it will be what it is supposed to be. I really think it's great when people find comfort in the concept that they have been saved and are going to Heaven. But for me, making my life be about getting myself to a place that I feel we are already in would make me into a caricature of the Cowardly Lion, chanting, "I do believe in spooks...I do, I do, I do!!" *** What is honest faith for many people would be an infantilizing self-deception on my part. I just can't go there.

Momzy: There are many beliefs and religions; none that are new. Just different names. No new gods...just new names. *** Christ threw down the gauntlet. Just read the accounts of the Pharisees and Sadducee's when Christ said there is only one way. They were waiting for a king who would release them from Roman occupation. They got a lowly carpenter who claimed equality with God. Here is the only message that saves. If you dig here....you will find eternal life....if you are looking for that treasure. 'I AM' (direct implication from Scripture of Christ's preexistence and deity see Exodus 3:14)—passages all from John: "the bread of life" 6:35
"the light of the world" 8:12 9:5
"the gate" 10:7
"the good shepherd" 10:11, 14
"the resurrection and life" 11:25
"the way, the truth and the life" 14:6
"the resurrection and life" 11:25
"the true vine" 15:1
This leaves no doubt as to where the true treasure can be found!

Again, Momzy, I appreciate, admire, and respect your understanding of the Message. I think we have both found our Treasure in different ways. I admit, though, I'm the kind of guy who keeps digging around the chest in hopes of finding other jewels that got scattered around. (Bad analogy, but what can you expect from a mere mortal?)

Momzy: We know that all the OT law, whether ceremonial, civil or moral was given for a reason. In Lev 1-4 we see a woman to be "ceremonially unclean" for a period of time, not dirty or sinful. Since Scripture interprets Scripture see Gen 1-27&28. God is the creator of sex. *** The Canaanite religions incorporated prostitution and immoral rites as people begged their gods to make their crops, herds, and families increase. Israel's religion avoided all sexual connotations. By keeping worship and sex entirely separate, God helped the Israelites avoid confusion with pagan rites. With regard to ceremonial law....Christ claimed his coming was the fulfillment of the law. Another reason they hung Him on the cross! Great example to use...thanks 'T'. *** Tony, I'll leave you with this one while you are still digging around for treasure. John 4:13-14 *"Jesus answered and said to her, 'Everyone who drinks of this water will thirst again; but whoever drinks of the water that I will give him shall never thirst; but the water that I will give him will become in him a well of water springing up to eternal life.'"* Matthew 7-8 *"Ask, and it will be given to you; seek, and you will find; knock, and it will be opened to you. For everyone who asks receives, and he who seeks finds, and to him who knocks it will be opened. 13 Enter through the narrow gate; for the gate is wide and the way is broad that leads to destruction, and there are many who enter through it. 14 For the gate is small and the way is narrow that leads to life, and there are few who find it."* You gotta dig in the right place and look for the right thing, 'T'. There will be no doubt if you find it.

Goodfella: And there's a big...no HUGE difference. If we are just trying to live the Bible principles or are we finding life through the Word of God. *** Here's what makes sense to me... Logically, if not but through nature alone, I believe there is a higher being that created. It does not make sense to see nature and believe it was accidental. If that higher being created us, there is a desire for relationship...not just create, leave, create, leave. *** From there, it makes sense as I look at the world that there is a disconnect between creation and that higher being. If that is true, it makes sense that we messed it up, not the higher being. For it to be corrected, the fix would be from the higher being instead of the lesser being. *** If that is true than I believe there is a truth about that higher being that He would want to be revealed and would be active in revealing it. Obviously that matches the Christian stance which, of course, makes logical sense to me as it is the only concept that matches that line of thought. *** In other words, if there is a truth... it's not a matter of what works or matches best for you... it's a matter of finding the truth as it is and then letting it shape us. For this reason, I cannot understand logically the thought process of finding what works for you (generic you, not targeting a specific person).

Goodfella, I completely understand your journey to God through Christ, and I think your logic is right on target given your starting premise: *"Logically, if not but through nature alone, I believe there is a higher being that created. It does not make sense to see nature and believe it was accidental. If that higher being created us, there is a desire for relationship...not just create, leave, create, leave."* Once this premise is in place, everything else you've deduced follows. *** But I'm not convinced that an ontological approach to the Divine is the best one (at least for me). I'm pretty sure you and Momzy understand what ontology is, but for those who may not, it is about God as Being. Being implies intellect, and it follows that if God is a Being, He has an intellect far superior to the creatures He created. In my late teens I left the Catholic Church because I simply could not find meaning within its rituals and theology (pre-Vatican II via Baltimore Catechism #3). After examining a number of other faiths and philosophies (one of my college minors), I realized there were more possibilities for approaching the Divine than my limited exposure through Catholicism—or even Christianity in general—allowed for. Thus, my eventual development of a non-ontological conceptualization of the Divine: God as process. *** Once I came to this point of awareness, I was able to look at a bigger picture concerning creation—one which can embrace other understandings of faith as parts of a much bigger Truth than any of us—with our limited capacity—will ever fully comprehend. It doesn't surprise me that most people watch the unfolding of the Cosmos and see patterns that suggest an Intellect at work. We see what we expect to see. We human beings have developed intelligence; therefore we are going to tend to read Intelligence into what we observe. Still, the longing to connect with a perceived Reality is genuine. I remember one time lying on my back and looking up into a clear night sky—in a place and time when the Milky Way was commonly visible—and having a momentary awareness of the vastness that I was such a minute part of. *** I later understood it as a God-experience—one in which I was absorbed in Awe—that overwhelming sense of fear and amazement and absorption. There was no recognition of intellect—more the sense that maybe a hypothetically self-aware drop of water might experience in being suddenly cognizant of the ocean. Those awareness moments are rare and sporadic in our lives, but I believe this is what most of us are after when we worship. And so religions are created by human beings to help us in large part to get to that sense of Connection. Of course, another component of many religions is to seek the answer to the question of the meaning of life and what happens after we die. As far as we know, we are the only specie on this planet that has a sense of its upcoming mortality and hence a need to ask those questions. *** Let me be clear: An ontological conception of the Divine is neither better nor worse than any other way to God. It is simply a different way—but one that, for me, opens up a wider understanding of my relationship with the Totality. Given this perspective, I can accept the limitations of both the scientific method and the spiritual approach to understanding the Creation and its wondrous expressions. The story of our Christian connect to God is only one possibility—one that has special significance for me since I have an epistemological grounding in our Judeo-Christian culture. But the more I study the historical development of our shared faith traditions, the better I feel about my decision to take a non-creedal approach to my learning, and that's what works for me. I would never suggest that it should work that way for everyone. This historical-critical approach does give me insight that only serves to strengthen my faith. *** I'll offer one small example: When reading the NT, there seems to be a discrepancy in the Gospels as to when Jesus was crucified. Matthew has Him on the cross on Passover whereas John clearly has Him dying before Passover begins. There have been rationalizations offered to try to reconcile these two accounts, but none of them hold up to close scrutiny. I personally don't think these differences constitute a discrepancy at all—they are simply different interpretations of the same event. If the Gospels are history, then we must ask the question: What really happened? That is a modern western approach to Scripture. The Jews who wrote the Gospels asked a different question—one that had been circulating in synagogues for decades before Mark put his account into writing: What did the Jesus experience mean? I think that by trying to understand the context for the Gospels' creation, we get closer to the reality of what the Jesus experience was/is all about.

Momzy: The Gospels are in complete harmony with each other. I find them amazing. As you well know, they describe some events in common but as seen through the eyes of different writers. Each Gospel has its own uniqueness as it give the accounts of the Lord Jesus Christ. Regardless of this, the picture it paints of Christ's divine nature and character are exactly the same in all four Gospels. In fact, you'll find absolutely no difference anywhere in the N.T. *** You know some of the ways I approach Scripture when interpreting. Let me make this statement again. While our copies of the Bible are not actually from the original or the inspired texts, the Holy Spirit superintended the preservation so that what we have is virtually inspired and adequate for the divine purposes for which they were preserved. *** 2 Timothy 3-16,17 *"All Scripture is inspired by God and profitable for teaching, for reproof, for correction, for training in righteousness; so that the man of God may be adequate, equipped for every good work."* *** If this isn't true, then the Bible is a hoax. If only part of the Bible is true, how do I know which part? If man wrote the Bible without divine inspiration, then it's just another good book and I can pick and choose what I like. *** Tony, I am trying to understand your perspective of what the Bible is and the authority you place on it. You know mine. And I'll be the first to admit that even in evangelical circles differences do exist.

My perspective of the Bible is that it is one of many holy books that exist in specific cultural milieus. From my western, Judeo-Christian perspective, it is perhaps the single most important book in terms of its impact on our understanding of human relationship with the Divine. But it is ultimately a book—written by God-inspired men reacting to specific cultural events over an approximate 1,100-year history. I both agree and disagree with you when you say, "*Each Gospel has its own uniqueness as it gives the accounts of the Lord Jesus Christ. Regardless of this, the picture it paints of Christ's divine nature and character are exactly the same in all four Gospels. In fact, you'll find absolutely no difference anywhere on the N.T.*" *** I agree with this statement as far as it goes. But the fact remains that the uniqueness you've cited paints a very different set of events and interpretations of Christ's nature and mission—so much so that it took over three centuries of developing internecine battles to settle the issue at the Council of Nicaea—and that was done by vote (which wasn't quite unanimous). For me, this only raises more questions. How should we understand the concept of the Bible being the "Word of God?" *** The canon of the NT was/is an ongoing process, and is varied in many different Christian denominations. Many Christian sects had their own versions of sacred texts. The process of establishing orthodoxy was often vicious and bloody. In the end, it was never really settled, as witnessed by the Reformation and the existence of multiple versions of the Bible today—including Eastern Orthodox, Coptic, Roman Catholic, KJV and its offshoots. I find the socio-political history of the development of this collection of sacred writings fascinating, but it doesn't convince me that your premise that "*the Holy Spirit superintended the preservation so that what we have is virtually inspired and adequate for the divine purposes for which they were preserved*" is one I can understand in the way you do, unless I come to that conclusion metaphorically. *** You cited 2 Timothy 3-16,17 "*All Scripture is inspired by God and profitable for teaching, for reproof, for correction, for training in righteousness; so that the man of God may be adequate, equipped for every good work.*" The problem for me in using internal proofs is that they create a circular definition: This book is inspired by God because it says it is. *** Personally, I agree that it is so inspired, but that doesn't mean that God verbally dictated it to the authors. The Koran makes that very claim, while the Bible does not. Since the inspiration of the authors is frequently open to interpretation, context—historical, linguistic, and literary—is critical to understanding what they are saying and why they are saying it. For instance, the very verses you cited here are from a letter purported to be written by Paul but which most Bible scholars over the past hundred years have concluded was written at least a half century after Paul's death. *** For me, the specific authorship of a Biblical text is less important than understanding what happens when contradictory messages are delivered in the name of the same author. If there are genuine Pauline letters and others produced later in his name (a common literary practice in Paul's day) then you often get conflicting messages from the passages. Did Paul support the institution of slavery and the second-class status of women? The genuine Pauline letters would appear to indicate a more egalitarian attitude on Paul's part, but many of the disputed letters and the Pastoral Letters (I & II Timothy and Titus) paint an opposite picture. So, do we need to discern what's going on if we're going to get "the Word of God" right? In my opinion, absolutely. *** You also said, *"If this [II Timothy] isn't true, then the Bible is a hoax. If only part of the Bible is true, how do I know which part. If man wrote the Bible without divine inspiration, then it's just another good book and I can pick and choose what I like."* I don't think that the Bible is less true because it contains apparent inconsistencies and contradictions. This is simply due to the varied authors living in varied times reacting to varied cultural conditions and events. We need to work hard to know what parts of it apply to us today and why they do. If the point of one's faith is to achieve Salvation, it seems to me that the Bible provides everything one might need for that purpose. If one sees the Process differently, there is still plenty of wisdom and understanding to be gleaned from its teachings. Jesus is the ultimate point of the NT. How one comes to God through Him is an individual thing. *** But let me pose this question: What if Jesus weren't Divine in the popular meaning of that word? What if the whole Son of God/Begotten of God/The Word Made Flesh concept was ultimately metaphorical? Would that make His teachings to us on how we should live our lives and treat each other any less true? Would we not try to live ethically and still seek a relationship with God? I think we all know the answer to that. Jesus taught us to live and love abundantly—to love God—and our neighbor—with all our hearts, minds, souls, and strength. If we do that, what else do we need? Reassurance that we're "saved?" Not me. I trust in the God Process too much to need constant reminders that I'm already there. *** Hope this helps clarify where I'm coming from, theologically speaking, Momzy.

Momzy: So, in your God process, as man evolved, he developed a conscience, or consciousness. By the way, that's just one of the things evolution cannot explain. Why did we get this and what purpose does it serve? The first man to have consciousness when he was still a cave man...knows something is different. But he has no concept of right or wrong. He knows nothing of God...Maybe he sees some other humans or ancestors who didn't quite make it to "reality." He goes over and cuts off their heads because they have some food he wants.

I don't think the development of a conscience is beyond the scope of evolutionary theory, although I don't know how far the study of it has progressed. But it raises the question of why human beings develop consciences—or a sense of compassion, love, faith, or a whole other set of intangible abilities for that matter. The simple reason is that higher brain function allows emotions to replace instincts. Emotions are simply programmable instincts, and in all animal groupings there are divisions. Primates build hierarchical social structures. Eventually we experiment with what works and what doesn't, and our ability to comprehend the Divine and use it as a social structuring tool goes through some evolution as well. By the way, that scenario you outlined for the caveman is pretty much the way Joshua and the

Israelites behaved when invading Palestine—which says more about their primitive understanding of God than it does about God (I hope) unless one takes the Bible literally.

Momzy: I submit to you, that in your God process, the first human, Fred Phelps, or Hitler's German people are no more guilty of sin than a lion when it kills its prey.

Not in the Process I describe as being accessible through Jesus by way of his ethical teachings—unless you want to argue that Phelps and/or Hitler were acting the way Christ taught us to. But if so, I'd like to know the Chapter and Verse on that one! ☺

Momzy: Because the measuring stick of right and wrong means something different to each person. We are all part of the cosmos, spiritually floating, like the ice chunk does with gravity. Good and evil exist only in the minds of those who perceive it! Who am I to force anyone to believe in right or wrong as I see it. I get my definitions from the Bible.

But, Momzy—don't we all get our measures of right and wrong, good and evil from the parameters of what our culture allows us knowledge about? Sure you get your moral direction from the Bible (but I bet from other places as well). So do I. Moral direction isn't dependent on the Bible, and a consensus of what's right and/or wrong can—and is—reached for any society from a diverse set of sources.

Momzy: And while I admire your God process, I feel that much of it came from your experience in the Catholic Church. If I grew up in South Central LA, had parents who were drug addicts and lived on the streets, what chance is there that I could make connection with your God process?

We all come to God/Process through our life experiences. There is no other way for that to happen. What difference does it make if a person comes to God some other way than yours or mine or no way at all?

Momzy: Therefore, I declare myself not guilty by reason of my environment when I rob a store to eat. Now take the poor kid in Mexico. He hauls drugs across the border so he can eat. He's not guilty of anything because he needs to eat. The measuring stick is different, isn't it? (By the way, that's how progressives think you know!)

As a progressive, the way I think would be more like this: There are conditions contributing to the behaviors of the two kids that need to be addressed if we, as a global community, want those actions to be minimized (we'll probably never stop them completely). The measuring stick has to take into account the severity of any behavior deemed undesirable by a society. This puts a lot of the responsibility for eliminating the causes of undesirable behavior on those privileged enough to have the wherewithal to impact positively on the problem. We ignore those causes at our own peril.

Momzy: I remember in an anthropology class discussing some tribe that still practiced cannibalism. We were taught there was nothing wrong with that because it was a cultural norm for them. Didn't matter that they worshiped a bamboo pole and hacked each other up for food. *** Hitler's Germany had cultural norms. Frodo has his norms. All created by man, each for different reasons. Defining good and evil...as each man is seen fit to do. God...is unable to communicate right or wrong, because God can more easily be defined as a process. As a matter of fact, evolution, another God process, would favor the Hitlers of the world as only the strongest survive.

Momzy, cannibalism doesn't work the way you describe—in the rare cases where it is still practiced in any form today. Social Darwinism has long been discredited—but if Hitler were the role model for its application, the best that can be said is that he came out on the losing side of that "argument." Here's the bottom line: You and I come to the Bible from different perspectives and that means we're going to see our post mortem end goals differently. But let me ask you a question my Philosophy 101 professor asked when the discussion turned—as it inevitably does for college freshmen in such classes—"If there were absolute proof that came to light tomorrow that God did not exist—would you act any differently than you would today?" The kid that robs a store or sells drugs or cheats on a test or has an abusive sexual relationship with someone isn't doing so because he hasn't heard of God or doesn't believe in God. He does so because it is the way he has defined his life's conflicts based on his cultural experiences. So, should we teach him what the Bible says, or should we provide for his material and emotional needs in ways that will reduce his perceived need to behave in socially undesirable ways. My answer: Why aren't we doing both? *** Momzy, I feel like you're trying to get a grip on my religious concepts in ways that will make sense according to your perception of Truth. I don't think that will work in the end because our approaches to Truth stem from different starting perspectives. That was inevitable the moment we were born two different people. I think the important thing—like I said to Goodfella earlier—is that we find reason to celebrate our commonalities (our very obviously shared ethical values) rather than worry over differences that are going to exist no matter how much we debate them. Just my opinion, of course.

Momzy: Does your God process have limitations or parameters? I know you mentioned living in harmony. But metaphorically speaking, what does that mean? For you, it means something different than it does for me. *** Without a fixed measuring stick that defines good and evil, how will good and evil be assessed? That is, if you even recognize good and evil in your reality.

Goodfella: Tony, I'm not sure I would call you a Christian in the way I define that word, but you do seem to be a seeker. When we are talking about God, a higher being.... Can we really expect to understand everything about Him? Is it about what we can prove and understand? Or is it about what He reveals about Himself to us and we trust?

You're right, Goodfella—I am a seeker, and I expect to be one all of my life. But I think there are two kinds of seekers in the world—those that are trying to fill a void in their spirits and those who are looking to increase their knowledge of how their faith works. I hope I have conveyed the seriousness with which I take my faith in God to establish myself as the second kind of explorer. *** I understand that from a certain perspective, what I'm saying would be considered a "false teaching" to those who come to the Bible from a fundamentalist approach. The Fundamentalist basic premises include: The Deity of Jesus, the Virgin Birth, the Blood Atonement, the Bodily Resurrection, and the inerrancy of the scriptures. *** On the other hand, to those who come to the Bible from a modernist approach, the Five Fundamentals can seem naïve or uninformed. I think there's a danger in this kind of labeling because it carries such negative connotations that it automatically becomes a conversation stopper. I understand that isn't the way you explained your use of the term, but let's be frank, some people do get carried away. To pp, for instance, I've moved from "false teacher" to an agent of Satan. Admittedly, he's on one end of a spectrum, but I've heard this before from a few others on these threads or in letters to the newspaper. Even accounting for their pushback to some of my less-than-charitable posts, this does border on the superstitious even from a normal Fundamentalist perspective. *** I worry about extremists in either camp because there is no honest discourse with them, and lack of communication leads to misunderstanding, and misunderstanding leads to mistrust, and mistrust leads to fear, and fear leads to hate. I have to believe that no matter what our theological differences are, we all know in our hearts that this is not the best way for us to be in the world with each other. *** I have a friend who is an ordained American Baptist minister who is also a lesbian. She tells a story about the first time she marched in a gay-pride parade. In a crowd of somewhere between 80,000 and 100,000 participants, there were about a dozen protesters standing on the sidelines. They held signs with the usual threats of hellfire and damnation if she and the other lesbians and gays who were marching didn't somehow transform themselves into heterosexuals. *** As she passed this small group, she was hit hard in the head by an object one of them threw at her. It sent her reeling, but she shook it off and bent down and scooped up the projectile, only to discover that it was a pocket edition of the Bible. Now, I doubt that protester had any intention of inflicting physical harm on anyone, but the extreme zeal that drives some people on matters of faith can often easily get out of hand.

Goodfella: I believe I'm on record saying that the church in some areas has not done well in reaching out in a loving way to the GLBT community. That protester is a good example of that failure to be loving.

Goodfella, my concern is that the kind of zeal that causes people to behave that way isn't just limited to gay pride protesters. I wonder if you remember about ten or so years ago when I'd just moved to this town and I asked the City Council if they could begin sessions with a moment of silent prayer instead of orally reciting The Lord's Prayer. I told them then and will say so now: I love that prayer and would happily join in saying it (and often do) with anyone in any appropriate setting. But our city is diverse, and that prayer is highly sectarian and—in that context—exclusionary to many. *** For a month, the newspaper was filled with letters of invective, and I even had a threat of physical damage to my home passed on to me through someone who wanted to warn me. That was the response from a "Christian" community to someone asking that the prayer format at a secular meeting be expanded to include all members of the community.

That's what the rhetoric of extremists can do to a community, but I'm heartened when Christians like you and Momzy and others are willing to engage in a dialogue that can be beneficial to all involved. If I've seemed combative on past threads, it's probably because, to some degree, I have been. My experiences with the Pistol Pete's of this town has shaped some of that, and the vandalism and physical violence that some of my friends, associates, and former students have suffered because of "Christian" hate rhetoric has made me wary of people who spout their invective then get upset when I call them on it. *** I had a similar experience with that kind of anti-gay hate mail that was being published regularly in the newspaper. Two very rabid regulars were a man named Elmer and another named John. As I engaged in a verbal slug-fest with both of these guys, it eventually dawned on me that—even though I was being regularly thanked by people who were offended by their verbal assaults—I wasn't really going to the heart of the matter which was the Scriptural authority on which most of the negativity was being based.

Goodfella: It's the "us" versus "them" mentality that we saw too often on the other threads. That's why I'm glad we are having this chance to have an honest discussion. I am still not sure how you see yourself in your journey to Christ, if that is what you believe you are doing.

I've spoken about some of my spiritual journey before. What I didn't describe was my earlier acquaintance with the Bible as an object of study. Growing up in a small Midwest town as a Catholic then going off to college and taking Philosophy 101, I was amazed to find out God was dead (apparently not as dead as Nietzsche is now, though). So I went through my perfunctory atheist stage—until I discovered the Bible could be read from a historical-critical perspective. *** For a while, when I was in the army, one of my nicknames was "Monk" because I was always reading the Bible. I've read all of it at least once and much/most of it many more times. I don't usually bother to memorize chapter and verse but I have copies of it in virtually every room of my house, and when someone does quote such to me, I tend to look it up to make sure I'm getting the whole context and not just the cherry-picked lines. I give all this background by way of saying that as I delved deeper into the supposed LGBT-related verses, they didn't seem to add up to what people were saying they did. But, I found Jesus' views to be spot on. The more I explored His ethical teachings, the more I came into an awareness of my own connectedness to the God Process through Him. *** That was over 10 years ago, and even though I've had 40+ years of exploring my spirituality in general, over the last decade, I've spent much of my non-employment related energies to studying my Christology specifically. As I said, I do not take my faith lightly. Now, all this has been prelude to an actual response to a specific question posed by you, Goodfella. You asked: *"When we are talking about God, a higher being…. Can we really expect to understand everything about Him? Is it about what we can prove and understand? Or is it about what He reveals about Himself to us and we trust?"* *** I once heard John Shelby Spong (retired Episcopal Bishop of Newark) respond to a question about how one should go about talking to an atheist about God. His response was: "I usually begin by telling him that the God he doesn't believe in is the same one I don't believe in, either." So, let me start on a common note: I think we'd both agree that it would be foolish to imagine that we could ever understand everything about God. I also think we'd agree that we can't prove anything about God and that we will probably only understand very little about the Divine—and that we have to trust in how He-She-It is revealed to us. Which brings us to the heart of the question within your question: How is God revealed to us? The Fundamentalist answer to this is pretty direct and uncompromising. One need only open the Bible to find the inerrant Word of God who has Revealed Himself progressively up through the time that He sent His only Begotten Son, Jesus Christ as a Sacrifice so that we may be redeemed and reunited with Him. I've got absolutely no argument with anyone who comes to God through this understanding. *** But lots of us folk out here believe there are other ways in which God is revealed. The main reason I sought a non-creedal church was so I didn't have to feel trapped into rationalizing those creeds by trying to make the language I used to understand the Divine match up with the language of the stated creed. So, I went with Unitarian Universalism as a faith community where I am fostered in an environment that is supportive of each individual's effort to understand the Truth on his or her own terms. This is probably contrary to the accustomed practice in most churches where a core set of belief statements must be adhered to and interpreted by a specific set of definitions. *** UU's probably have a more varied list of resources for Divine revelation than many (even Modernist) Christians, but I'm not one for leaving any stone unturned in my quest for understanding.

UU's draw from:

A) Direct experience of that transcending mystery and wonder [of those] forces which create and uphold life;

B) words and deeds of prophetic women and men which challenge us to confront powers and structures of evil with justice, compassion, and the transforming power of love;

C) wisdom from the world's religions which inspires us in our ethical and spiritual life;

D) Jewish and Christian teachings which call us to respond to God's love by loving our neighbors as ourselves;

E) humanist teachings which counsel us to heed the guidance of reason and the results of science, and warn us against idolatries of the mind and spirit; and

F) spiritual teachings of earth-centered traditions which...instruct us to live in harmony with the rhythms of nature.

So, if we start with the 1st Fundamental—that the Bible is the inerrant Word of God—then the other four follow with precision and logic by today's interpretation of the meaning of the Cross (which I still contend wasn't Paul's view, but that's another discussion). The problem for me with this approach is that there is so much socio-political history that went into to developing the varied versions of that "inerrant Word" that are in use even today, that we really need some criteria on which to base our judgments as to which is the correct "inerrancy."

Goodfella: Why can't we just take it to Jesus' words since we seem to have a common denominator there? For example, Jesus said to Nicodemus, "I tell you the truth, no one can see the Kingdom of Heaven unless he is born again." To say that Jesus was great but there are other paths would be to say Jesus was a liar...Paul puts it this way, "That if you confess with your mouth, "Jesus is Lord," and believe in your heart that God raised him from the dead, you will be saved. For it is with your heart that you believe and are justified, and it is with your mouth that you confess and are saved." *** I don't for a moment believe Jesus was a liar, but to say we accept the words John or any other of the Gospel writers may have put into His mouth or we're calling Him one is, I believe a false choice.

One thing all versions of the Bible have in common is their record in the Gospels of Jesus as a real person who lived, taught, and was put to death in the 1st Century CE. For the Fundamentalist, there is no difference in one Gospel to the next, thematically speaking. The message is consistent in all four. The Modernist reads these books differently—that they are different perspectives on many of the same events, but that they draw different conclusions about the nature of Jesus. I don't argue that either the Fundamental or the Modern approach is better than the other—just that they're different. (We'll probably disagree on that, too, but that's what makes this thread so interesting.) You quoted Jesus speaking to Nicodemus which is of course, from

John. A Fundamentalist will take those words as literal, and maybe they are. But, a modernist will look at that and consider some or all of the following:

1) Did Jesus speak Greek? It's possible, but so often he is quoted from the Aramaic we need to consider that maybe he didn't. Greek was a common enough language in Jesus' times, and while it was the written language for the educated classes, Jesus hardly came from one of those families. Still, Nazareth was walking distance from Sepphoris and he might have been bilingual if he worked his carpenter's trade in that city. The reason the language he spoke is important is that *"born again"* is a play on words only in Greek. It would have not been said by Jesus if he only spoke Aramaic.

2) Since John was writing his Gospel 65-70 years after Jesus' death, and he doesn't seem to be using the Synoptics as a source, where is he getting such specific details of this conversation? There are all kinds of possibilities: Someone overheard the exchange and passed it on, Nicodemus might have told John or someone else and they passed it on, etc. But there's no way to know for sure, and given the tone and theme of John's Gospel, it is just as likely that he was more intent on making a theological point that recording actual history. (A Modernist would see nothing wrong in this—it was a way of making a very significant point of theology after the Followers of the Way had been barred from the synagogues.) Don't forget, the bar Kochba revolt was less than 30 years down the road from John, and that last attempt by a "Messiah" to break the Roman yoke would seal the schism between Jews and Christians forever.

3) When John opens his Gospel with the absolutely lyrical description of Logos, he is making a statement about the nature of the Christ that goes far beyond the statements made by the other three Gospel writers. He is saying that the nature of Jesus was unmistakably Divine. But fully Divine AND fully human? This

is so unsettled by the Scriptures that religious wars (vicious, bloody slaughters) were fought over the issue up through the 6th and 7th Centuries. And then, the Modernist will ask: How was that Divine nature perceived? As a Jew, John would not have perceived the Father and Son to be one and the same. Even where Jesus is made to appear to be saying this, the concept of Logos tells us that He is not saying what our 21st Century minds tend to read into those words. *** So, how is the Logos different to the 1st Century CE mind than it is to us today? The answer is relatively simple by analogy. The Logos is to God just as the written page is to the author. Is the intent of the author (assuming literary competence on the author's part) recorded on that page? Is the creative expression of the author on that page? Are the author's ideas and mindset reflected on that page. The answer to all these questions is Yes. But is that written page the author? Obviously not. Like all analogies about God, this one has its limitations, but it does go to a mindset more in keeping with a Jewish John reacting to a culture in which his own people are rejecting a Messiah he has come to know and love. From a Modernist Christian perspective, John is probably the least historically accurate Gospel—but probably the most spiritually expressive one for the emerging faith that would be known as Christianity.

Goodfella: If we start questioning what parts of Scripture we can take as literal but reject other parts as something else—say a metaphor or something—doesn't that call into question Jesus' authority?

I suppose it depends on what one feels his authority is. I think I know what you want me to explain, Goodfella, and I hope I'm understanding what you are saying to me correctly. If not, I'm open to instruction. But you cited what John said that Jesus said, followed by *"To say that Jesus was great but there are other paths would be to say Jesus was a liar...Paul puts it this way, 'That if you confess with your mouth, "Jesus is Lord," and believe in your heart that God raised him from the dead, you will be saved. For it is with your heart that you believe and are justified, and it is with your mouth that you confess and are saved.'"* *** I don't for a moment believed Jesus was a liar, but to say we either accept the words John or any other of the Gospel writers may have put into His mouth or we're calling Him one, is, I believe, (as you stated) a false choice. *** One of my occasional hobbies is performing magic shows for kids. One of the basic tools of magic is the Magician's Choice. You get to pick from a set of options that defines the limits of the illusion being performed and is already set to "force" a selection. A while back there was a book out that—with apparently flawless logic—led the reader to such a choice: Jesus was either a liar, a lunatic, or the Lord (in this case meaning a Messiah interchangeable with God). But the choices were rigged to produce the conclusion the author wanted the reader to reach. His technique was obvious for a lot of reasons, but his conclusions were based on a limited set of choices. But they couldn't stand up to scrutiny if the reader factored in an understanding of the use of the word *Lord* in Paul's day along with an understanding of Paul's reaction to the Roman state religion that was broadcast on every temple erected to exalt a glorious Emperor, *"Son of God, Lord, and bringer of peace."* *** Romans proclaimed the divine to be manifest in military strength which led to victory and then to peace whereas Paul deliberately stood in defiance to this by proclaiming Jesus as Lord, in which the order of things was: the divine leading to justice and righteousness and then to peace. Any wonder he got arrested so many times? For Paul, Christ crucified was a shorthand statement every Follower of the Way understood. The wisdom of the world (the empire) killed Jesus. God made that a gift to mankind, not so they'd go to Heaven, but so that people could come to be in Christ (get a spiritual transplant as Crossen and Borg would say) and be born again into a life renewed in Spirit. The wisdom of the world killed Christ, but God raised Him up to glory as a sign that the "foolishness of God" could make a mockery of the "wisdom of the world." *** I'll stop for now with this last question for those out there still following this post to ponder: Is there anything I have said about the Modernist approach to Scripture and/or Christianity that would preclude anyone—myself included if I were to interpret my spiritual life in a different way than I do now—from saying, "I accept Jesus Christ as my personal Savior. I am born again in Him?" I don't think so. All I've been saying is that for some of us, there is another way to God through Jesus, and for other people in other cultures, there are ways to God from their perspectives. *** Sorry this took so long—but the nature of Truth? That's a lot of ground to even begin commenting on.

Goodfella: Even if we just go off of Jesus' words in the gospels as a whole, written by firsthand and secondhand accounts by people involved, during a time when there were plenty of firsthand eye witnesses that could have verified or denied the claims.... Many of the things you are teaching do not match up to the Bible. I believe the claiming of being a Christian but not holding to the Word or His teachings completely is what challenges your talks with others. The Scripture shows us the path to salvation and that it is singular through Christ...it is a false teaching to claim Christianity but teach a different version of it.

Goodfella, I'd like to respond to some of your (and Momzy's) premises. First, let me say that the inconsistencies found in the four Gospels are, at times, more than minor when it comes to determining the nature of a Jewish Jesus at a specific time and place in history. That they differ speaks more to the Reality of Jesus and the God experience his followers felt in Him than if they had been verbatim (creedal) accounts. But before it was assembled in its present forms, the Bible was a series of manuscripts that were developed into a politically determined, authorized set of writings that formed a somewhat fluid canon. Multiple Christianities competed with each other (and still do), but, in the end, some of them emerged as mainstream orthodoxy. These still-practiced Christianities more or less say the same thing about the nature of Jesus, but they still differ on many points. What is salvation—especially since our modern interpretation of Paul is colored by which Paul we're speaking of—the one who wrote the seven confirmed authentic letters and maybe some of the disputed ones or the Paul who wrote the Pastorals (I and II Timothy and Titus)? What was the significance of his interpreting the Christ experience as "Jesus is Lord" and "Christ crucified" and would these terms have any meaning without an occupying Roman Empire? Indeed, would there have even been Christianity without Rome? *** So what makes the Bible "God revealed to us and is the Holy Book" in its present forms? Even today, what is considered canon depends on one's sect; whether or not salvation is obtained through works alone, faith alone, or a combination thereof is an evolution of conflicting thought that began in the Reformation, continued through the Thirty Years War, and is still being debated today. Paul and the Gospel writers have been continuously reinterpreted to produce our modern 21st Century understanding of what they wrote. We don't read them from a 1st Century Jewish perspective to understand how and why these writings were produced. And, even though their meanings have constantly been debated and reinterpreted over the past two millennia, we insist that there is a one-size-fits-all way to grasp the Truth of their revelations. The language of the Scriptures reflects an understanding of Jewish culture as it was affected by time and place. The world-shaping events that impacted a tribal people who understood themselves to be chosen by God ultimately resulted in the elevation of their account of their evolving understanding of God to the status of Supreme Authority for a faith the original Patriarchs could have never envisioned. This doesn't make the Bible unimportant or irrelevant. On the contrary; it makes it all the more remarkable for its emergence as the primary source for millions of people to access the God experience. But not to place Scripture—and its writers—into their historical contexts is to open oneself to gross misinterpretation of their messages.

Goodfella: I've stated before that in my authority as a pastor, I am accountable to teach the truth to the best of my ability, and I cannot see how that would be possible if I didn't believe the Bible is completely inerrant. If I were to deny that, what could make any new interpretation of its text anything more than my own teaching and not God's?

Good question. I believe it is the duty of those of us who call ourselves Christians to constantly explore what those meanings are and to continuously reinterpret them in the light of advances in our knowledge of how our universe works. Goodfella, you said, *"I believe the claiming of being a Christian but not holding to the Word or His teachings completely is what challenges your talks with others."* I understand and respect where you're coming from, but not all Christians have a problem with what I'm saying—in fact, my views are based on similar understandings by prominent Christian scholars. You also said, *"The Scripture shows us the path to salvation and that it is singular through Christ...it is a false teaching to claim Christianity but teach a different version of it."* Again, I understand your viewpoint and take no offense with your opinion. I hope you will take my answer in the same spirit. *** To declare one set of writings as the "official Word of God" then argue that the only way to the Truth and/or Salvation is by the way those writings are "officially" interpreted is to create a circular argument. I'm not saying it's wrong, only that it will have meaning exclusively for those that accept the original premise. By that definition, everything that contradicts or even holds up to serious question the original premise must, *ipso facto*, be a "false teaching." The problem I have (from a logical perspective) is that this implies that there really is no other way for a person to come to God through Jesus except the "authorized" way. I have to reject that idea, if for no other reason than I am my own living proof that this isn't the case. This is true to so many other people in the same position I'm in that they often react with anti-fundamentalist attitudes that put so many conservative Christians on the defensive. I know this "my way or the highway" attitude was a longtime barrier to my reconnection with Jesus, and that it took my engagement with LGBT justice issues to bring me back to Christianity.

Goodfella: I do not agree that some letters were of Paul authentic, some weren't, and whatnot. While the author of Hebrews is debatable as is does not claim an author, there is nothing to hint otherwise on the others. In all honesty, in my decades of study, I have not even heard that suggested (as well as several other statements you have offered).

Momzy: Momzy's turn again. First, I am curious what you mean as fundamental mainstream Christianity? Surprisingly, I don't consider myself a fundamentalist. To those whose rigid orthodoxy condemns anyone outside of their type of clan, I would consider fundamentalist. I try not to condemn anyone. I am doing a paper and one of the questions is "What does the Bible say about the divine nature of Christ?" I am interested in how you would answer this question. *** The other thing I am interested in is how one will know if they are on wrong path in their God process as you describe it. As an example in my case, I cannot fathom how one of my family members can claim to be a Christian, go to church umpteen times a week, and openly degrade minorities on a regular basis. *** The thing I want to know about the God process, or anyone else's if they want to chime in, is what drives anyone to a conviction that the process/path they are on is indeed the correct one. *** This is a serious question for all of us. Some Muslims take the resources available in their religion and strap bombs to themselves as a sign of faith. In other religions, Buddhist etc., they throw prayers and throw gifts to manmade statues (gods).

Mike: Momzy, I really have nothing to offer on the Christian discussion currently underway, but can answer your question. I arrived upon my religious path through need-induced investigation and the resonance of what I found upon the chords of my spirit.

Mine is essentially experiential, although ritual, prayers, morality, ethics, ceremonies and study are critical to my moving forward with it. As for my conviction that my path is the correct one, I am, based upon experiences, outcomes, and station in life, convinced that it is the CORRECT ONE FOR ME. I am equally convinced that it is not the path for most.

Hey, Momzy—before I start I just want to point out what I'm pretty sure you know already: Most Muslims don't resort to violence any more frequently than most Christians do. And idolatry to one person may be the same as beseeching intercession with God through a prayer to Mary or a saint to another. Some even turn the Bible into an idol of sorts. *** That said, I've identified 4 questions that you've raised that I think are terrific topics for discussion. They are as follows:

1) What is fundamental mainstream Christianity?

2) What does the Bible say about the divine nature of Christ?

3) How does one know if they are on wrong path in their God process as I describe it?

4) What drives anyone to conviction that the process/path they are on is indeed the correct one?

I'll give my take on these one at a time, acknowledging that other people's opinions will differ. I would describe fundamental mainstream Christianity (as opposed to plain old ordinary Christianity—both Catholic and mainline Protestant denominations, i.e. Methodist, Episcopal, Lutheran, Presbyterian, etc.) as members of those church communities who attest to being "Bible-believing," born again, evangelical worshipers whose main understanding of the purpose of their faith is to get them into Heaven. Just as a reminder: A Fundamentalist is usually defined as someone adhering to five basic premises I listed before: The Deity of Jesus, the Virgin Birth, the Blood Atonement, the Bodily Resurrection, and the inerrancy of the Scriptures. *** I'm not using any part of the above description pejoratively. How and what people believe is quite okay with me as long as it doesn't single out other people for demonization and diminishment. Anti-Semitism would be one kind of behavior that would make me challenge the tenants of professed faith that lead a "true" believer to such conclusions. My record on LGBT justice issues goes to that point as well. *** That said, there are plenty of mainstream Christians (I suspect the majority of them) who fall into the definition I've just given who practice a sincere form of their faith that is welcoming and inclusive of other beliefs. I admire and honor their embrace of Jesus' ethical teachings. We hold that in common. I refer to mainstream fundamentalism as opposed to non-mainstream conservative movements such as Mormons, Messianic Jews, etc. who are drawn indirectly from traditional fundamentalist approaches. That said, the issue of what the Bible says about the nature of Christ is something I think is less clear than Fundamentalists would acknowledge. There is an old philosophy joke that goes like this:

Jesus is standing with Simon Peter and Paul Tillich, the Christian existential theologian/philosopher.
Jesus asks Peter, "Who am I?"
Peter answers, "You are the Christ; the Son of God."
Jesus then asks Tillich the same question, to which he replies, "You are the Wholly Other; the Ground of Being."
Jesus looks at him and says, "Huh?"

I suspect that if Jesus were to ask the Apostle Paul what it meant to be the Son of God and then ask that same question of many mainstream Christians today, he'd reply to them as he did to Paul Tillich in the joke. "Huh?" *** The question has real meaning—who was Jesus historically speaking, and who is He to us today? I contend that these may be two very different things for a lot of people. At the very least, I think Paul understood Him in a very different way than most Christians do now. *** Let me be clear in stating that from a historical perspective, I understand Jesus as an apocalyptic Jewish teacher who delivered a message that would prepare humanity for the Kingdom of God on Earth. He taught that once the Son of Man appeared—which was eminent—the Kingdom of God would be instituted so we had all better start behaving the way we would once it was a done deal. Jesus thought the establishment of the Kingdom would occur within the lifetimes of some of his followers. So did Paul for that matter. Obviously, they got it wrong. Now I know that will sound like heresy to many people, but really, is it inconsistent with a fully human Jesus that maybe he'd be subject to human error from time to time? I mean, how godly is it to curse a fig tree for not bearing fruit out of season? Unless, of course, such actions are part of a story first told in the synagogues to make a point about something other than a barren tree?

Momzy: The "curse" of the fig tree was a judgment. Jesus was teaching a lesson about what happens to people who outwardly appear to observe his Law (the tree had leaves but no fruit), but they lacked true faith. He was showing what the end would be for the faithless (fruitless).

I understand the symbolic message, but if we read the Gospels in the order they were written, with Mark first, followed by Matthew, Luke, and John (with Acts inserted between Luke and John since it was the second half of Luke's work) then we can see a progression of thought about what Jesus' life was actually all about. All three of the synoptic are products of the synagogue and are written as readings to follow the Jewish liturgical calendar. The earliest, Mark, appears right about the time of the destruction of the Temple, when the oral tradition of Jesus is passing out of the living memory of those who were actually around in Jesus' lifetime. If the understanding of Jesus as the fulfillment of the older Jewish prophesies is to be preserved, there had to be a written record to be presented with the selections of the Torah (and possibly in place of or concurrent with the writings of the prophets) that were being read as part of the worship ritual. Mark covers about nine months of the liturgical year. Matthew extends his account to cover the entire year, occasionally correcting Mark and focusing his narrative on Jesus as the new Moses. Where Mark sparingly uses the term "Son of Man"—read Messiah—Matthew is quite clear in deeming Jesus as such. The term "Son of God" did not, by a long shot, carry the same weight in reference to the Messiah in Jesus' day. Son of God was a title given to Augustus, and when used in Jewish culture, it referred to a person or persons (or a nation) doing the will of God. Son of Man came from Daniel and referred to the transforming person who would intercede in Jewish affairs on God's behalf. *** The question we need to ask is: What was the Messiah (Son of Man; the Christ) supposed to be for the Jews of Jesus' time? To answer that, we have to remember that the cultural identity of the Chosen People was bound up in a remembrance of their former glory under David. Now they were a subject people, but at one time things had been very different. *** The Hebrew prophets had, from even before the Babylonian Captivity, been regularly predicting that a leader would come—a descendant of David—who would restore the kingdom to its former glory. *** By the end of Herod's reign in 4 BCE, claimants for the honor were already starting to appear with some frequency. There were reasons—obvious to us now from the historical perspective of two by-gone millennia—why the Jews were never going to have a chance to make this happen, but at the time of Jesus' appearance on the scene, there were enough people wanting to believe it could happen that the Jews would eventually risk the revolt that led to their last major Diaspora—the scattering of them as a people. *** Now, there were some idealists of that time who felt that the Kingdom of God—an actually earthly kingdom—would be ushered in through the spiritual—not military—efforts of God's anointed emissary. The nation would become an example of how to live within the framework of God's laws, and that example would transform the world. *** By the time of Jesus' birth, many components of these two concepts—that of the restored political kingdom and that of the earthly example leading to a nation steeped in God's law— had merged to varying degrees among rival religious and political factions. This is why John the Baptist was doing his thing in the Jordan and why many people thought he was the Messiah. And there were others, most of who, like John, were put to death for perceived acts of sedition. *** So, here comes the dilemma for Jesus' followers who see him as the prophesied Messiah. How does one accomplish God's mission if you've been executed as a criminal? No one expected the Messiah to be equal to God—that was never in the job description. Indeed, it would have been blasphemy to make such a claim, even if it had been in the realm of mental possibilities for any Jew—including Jesus—to think that way. *** The solution to this dilemma becomes apparent when one follows the authentic letters of Paul and the Gospels/Acts in their written—not published— order. Jesus as Messiah is progressively revealed to be God's Anointed One (the Christ). Mark's original Gospel is addressed to a community concerned with the destruction of the Temple. The original ends at 16:8— "…and they said nothing to anyone, for they were terrified." By the time Luke/Acts is written, the rift between synagogue and Followers of the Way was pretty much complete, and Luke has provided an alternative to reading the traditional Hebrew Scriptures in worship with his two-part story. But even in Luke, the idea that a Messiah announced by angels is interchangeable with God is never postulated. Son/Father did not equate as equals in the concept of Jesus' mission. But, by the time John composes his Gospel, there is no question of the divine nature of Jesus. He is The Word incarnate.

Goodfella: Just because Matthew and Luke had more material in their Gospels than Mark doesn't mean they all didn't believe that Jesus was divine. They are quite clear that they did.

I'm not sure I would agree with that, Goodfella. The point to all this is that just what the nature of Jesus was to the writers who gave us what was to become NT canon is varied and progressive. It is even more so with Paul. Given the flat earth cosmology of the ancients, the Jewish concept of Messiah and the Kingdom of God, added to the way Paul indicates he understand the resurrection to be non-physical—the New Testament synoptics and Paul's letters seem to suggest that its writers viewed Jesus as a human being by birth and made Divine by mission—and not by possession of Divine identity at birth. Except for John's gospel, of course, but given what came before him, it's easy to see a progressive revelation of the nature of Christ drawn from earlier Christian thinking, perhaps with a touch of Gnosticism mixed in. *** This, in my opinion, does nothing to diminish the power of Jesus' teachings or to negate the possibility to entering into the God Process by accepting His Truths. If the only reason a person accepts those teachings is because they think they are dictates from God through Jesus, I think that does dishonor to Him.

Momzy: I agree. There are people who profess their faith when really all they are looking for is a "Get out of Hell Free" card. Kind of like a barren fig tree, Huh?

☺ Momzy, I'm going to take a crack at the last two questions you posed and see if I can answer them as briefly as possible. *"So, how [does] one know if they are on wrong path in their God process as [I] describe it?"* I think the answer for me is obvious. Often, my life feels broken—spiritually incomplete. I bet the same is true for you and every other person of faith. We know when our actions make us feel less than decent and fully human. And every such action can be traced to a violation of the principle of unconditional love that Jesus taught us to have for each other. *** The second question about what drives anyone to conviction that the process/path they are on is indeed the correct one—I think Mike has answered as well as anyone could. Just as I don't think we need a checklist to determine when we are doing something we know to be wrong, I suspect each of us knows when the path we are on is resonating with and in the God Process. Unless one is a psycho- and/or sociopath, of course. *** I've stated before that I am an existentialist—which means that I believe that each of us defines our own purpose in life. When I was a Catholic, Baltimore Catechism #3 asked the question, "Why did God make us?" and answered, "God made us to know, love, and serve him so we could share happiness with Him in Heaven." That probably works as something literal for a lot of people, but not for me. I believe our purpose in life is self-determined. We are defined through conflict. All life is. But human beings have choices about which conflicts they decide to engage in. Even victims who have violence thrust on them have choices as to how to respond—until they are no longer physically or mentally capable of doing so. Good and evil exist as measuring tools to help in our decisions for what conflicts we will choose to engage in and how we will engage. But for each of us, they exist in relation to our experiences and development. In any society, there will be overlapping agreement by most people on what comprises either good or evil, and even those agreements are subject to debate and change.*** For me, the Process exists—if there are parameters, I can't know them because they will be beyond my limited human comprehension. But, I do know that there is direction, and that is governed by our willingness to move toward connection with It. I've found it to be quite impossible to do so while engaging in attitudes and behaviors that run contrary to the ethics Jesus defined for us in terms of how we should treat each other. Fred Phelps doesn't do this. Instead, he engages in behaviors just the opposite. It doesn't much matter that he claims to be speaking for God. We see examples of people doing that all the time. Talk is cheap, and all the vehemence we attach to our words—claiming Scriptural authority for them, but using them to diminish the lives of others, is pretty much a clue that one is not in the Process—at least for that moment. *** I do believe that our awareness of our connection to the Process comes in momentary fragments at best. We simply can't live our lives in that I-Thou relationship (to borrow Martin Buber's phrase) constantly. We live in a world that is physical and demands our attention to cope with it. That coping is the price we pay for being alive. It is conflict, but as human beings we get some choices as to how we will deal with challenges, and those choices give our lives definition and meaning. Some people never rise above the childish conflicts of school-yard drama, others occupy their lives in the pursuit of career or the acquisition and/or application of knowledge. Some attach to their work or to social causes—but all of us choose our own definitions. We also decide on what we think good and evil is. *** For me, good is that which betters my fellow brothers and sisters and the Earth on which we live.

Goodfella: Hey Tony, I know that often we type things and say something to the effect that "It won't surprise you I feel that way." In a way, I am surprised at a few of the things you have been typing the last couple days. Instead of going through point by point, let me ask a question at the root of things to get a better perspective of your foundation. *** I have been working under the assumption that you are a Christian with a very different view on a "sin" issue that you are passionate about. Is that correct? Let me better ask that...*** Are you a Christian? If so, how do you define what a Christian is (how do you become one? what does it look like?)

Thanks for the question Goodfella—you, too, Momzy. Yes, I identify as a Christian. I define a Christian as one who comes to the God Process through his/her application of the teachings of Jesus Christ as the ethical connection between themselves and others. Since I view all of us as in the Process, that which connects us to what Unitarian Universalists call "the interdependent web of life"—connects us to each other and God. Jesus showed us how to do that, and I believe that his message of a world transformed by love was and is so powerful that his followers back then as well as today recognized the Living God Process in him. I know this isn't fundamental mainstream Christianity, but it is a view shared by many progressive Christian theologians. I've named at least one who is very accessible to the non-scholar—John Shelby Spong. *** Again, I realize that how I come to God through Christ isn't traditional—at least tradition as established in the 11th Century when Paul's concept of salvation as a way to a spiritual place called Heaven through the Crucifixion was given its current status in the works of Anselm. Again, what I am learning about Paul (see Borg and Crossen, "The First Paul") keeps reinforcing my understanding of the meaning of Christ's message and the opportunity He provided for us to have atonement—think of the wordplay, at-one-ment—with God. The resurrected Christ to Paul was not likely a physical resuscitation. It was a resurrection of the self to be reborn again as a whole person "in Christ." I'm not sure my 21st Century mind would use all of Paul's terminology, but I believe the kind of Christianity I practice—one based on egalitarianism and the possibility of a Kingdom of God here on Earth is closer to where Jesus and Paul were coming from. *** Sin is that which separates us from God and therefore from each other. When we remain indifferent to the suffering of others; when we single others out for persecution; when we treat our Mother Earth as a trash heap; when we fail to reproduce responsibly; when we fail to seek all the possibilities for peace for everyone in this world—we are committing grievous sins (in my opinion). When our concern for our own souls making it to a happy place when we die outweighs our concern is that peoples of color, peoples of different ethnicities, LGBT people, non-Christian people, etc. get treated with equity and justice—well, in my opinion we are so far removed from what an actual Christian ought to look like that we need to be doing major work on our understanding of our spiritual priorities. I know the Protestant tradition is that we are saved by faith alone, but professions of faith ring hollow if we are all talk without action. That's my God-as-Infinitive analogy coming out: God is the "to," our actions complete the verb. *** Momzy; Goodfella—I can't imagine that we are very far apart ethically speaking. You both have been a pleasure to engage with, and I'm more than happy to keep it going.

Goodfella: Tony, I am glad that we have been able to talk so well these past few weeks and I think you will take the following in the heart it is intended. I do not mean it as a personal judgment (especially since I do not know you) but I do mean it as a determination by following the Scripture. *** What you are describing is not the teaching of the Bible in the area of being a Christian. Many of the things that you hold to as far as serving, loving, and giving to others are fruits that need to be showing in the life of one who has accepted Christ are very Biblical but they are not the path. *** The Scripture shows us the path to salvation and that it is singular through Christ. The fact that our salvation is through acknowledging with your mouth that Jesus is the Son of God (thus giving Him leadership) and believing in your heart He died and rose again (thus accepting His forgiveness) is taught in the Scripture. *** Our responsibility to love is taught within Christ's teachings in the Scripture as is His determination to do so through truth. The teaching of an afterlife, Heaven and hell are not added by any group, council, or person over the centuries, they are point blank teachings in the Scripture. The traditional way of looking at things for the most part is traditional because it is point blank the way it is. *** The Bible is God revealed to us and is the Holy Book (not one of many holy books that we can find which work best for us). It is one thing to pick minor points in the gospels from four different writers that don't matter to the major points and call them inconsistencies. It's another to compare different religious books of completely different religions and say that they are different options for different people to "truth." *** To say you are a Christian and not embrace all of His revelations and clear words does not compute. *** If you said you were not a Christian but was talking about Christianity as a study, I'm with you in the conversation. If you say there is no afterlife or truth but anyone can pick and choose what they want from any and all religions to make themselves feel better while waiting to become dust again, then still I could understand (though disagree). *** But, you are speaking of a religion that is about what you do instead of what He has done. My good works are a response to my gratitude for His grace within His physical death and resurrection, not a way to connect with us through my actions here with some kind of Heaven on earth. To put it in the strictest of terms, it is a false teaching to claim Christianity but teach a different version of it. *** I don't mean to be going on a rant and I appreciate you letting me type all this out. I wanted to wait until I gave you a full chance to explain what you wanted in this area for myself and others to understand where you are coming from. *** Tony, you remind me of Saul. He was a religious (though I would tag you more spiritual than religious) man who spent great energy being at the top of his class in knowledge and diligent in pursuing his cause. However, he completely missed the physical risen Christ and the one true path open to Him by what Christ had done. It is my prayer that you, like him (in his process to being renamed Paul as a true follower of Christ) have that experience where you come to the Lord through His path instead of your own.

Goodfella, I thank you for the exchanges we've shared. As I said in a previous post to you and Momzy, I know my theology embraces the paths you both have taken...I'm not so sure yours are able to stretch wide enough to embrace mine—but, then, they don't need to. * I say that humbly and I have no problem with knowing that you cannot embrace me as a fellow Christian. But—and again I say this as humbly as I can—in the end, it is given to no other person to say who or what I am. From my perspective, the approach to God through Jesus is a lot more intricate and interesting—and a lot more emotionally satisfying to me—than anything traditional Christianity ever had to offer. Meanwhile, I'll keep tripping down my Damascus road, not seeking to persecute my fellow Christians, but seeking them out to expand our praise of God with love that is inclusive of everyone. *** I fully acknowledge that I am a work in progress: Witness my exasperation with Pistol Pete on the God vs. Gays**

posts. One of the reasons I found myself going to the dark side in my responses to him was because he seemed so implacable in his pronouncements. It's not that you and Momzy do or don't agree more with his Christology than mine, but the both of you have engaged in what I recognize as the kind of behaviors in your exchanges with me that I believe Christ taught us to do. I've been treated with respect by both of you, and that's where I believe all connects to God should begin. It's what I recognize as Christian behavior—but then, I suspect it is the kind of behavior all people of genuine faith or ethical humanism would practice. *** I recognize my sin is that I'm all too ready to confront what I perceive as bullying by lashing back. Well, we all have work to do on ourselves, and this is my cross to bear. But, I have found these exchanges with you and Momzy worthwhile, and I do hope we will one day meet and know each other better. Thanks for the dialogue.